Christopher M. Lyman   Introduction by Vine Deloria, Jr.

THE VANISHING RACE

PHOTOGRAPHS OF INDIANS

AND OTHER ILLUSIONS

BY EDWARD S. CURTIS

Smithsonian Institution Press, Washington, D.C.

This book has been published in conjunction with the exhibition *The Vanishing Race and Other Illusions: A New Look at the Work of Edward Curtis*, organized and circulated by the Smithsonian Institution Traveling Exhibition Service

Front cover: *On the War-Path—Atsina* [79].
Back cover: *Cheyenne Warriors* [81]
Frontispiece: *A Blackfoot* [5]

Library of Congress Cataloging in Publication Data
Lyman, Christopher M.
The vanishing race and other illusions.
''Published in conjunction with the exhibition . . . organized and circulated by the Smithsonian Institution Traveling Exhibition Service''—Verso t.p.
Bibliography: p.
Includes index.
Supt. of Docs. no.: SI 1.2:In2/4
1. Indians of North America—Pictorial works—Exhibitions. I. Title. II. Curtis, Edward S., 1868–1952. III. Smithsonian Institution. Traveling Exhibition Service.
E77.5.L95   970.004′97   81-607152
ISBN 0-87474-622-1   AACR2

CONTENTS

ACKNOWLEDGMENTS

Without the support and confidence of countless individuals and institutions, this project would certainly have run amok in the labyrinth between conception and publication.

The research, which eventually led to this book, began several years ago with encouragement from Dr. Alan Trachtenberg, Professor of American Studies at Yale University. The award of a grant from the Youthgrants Program at the National Endowment for the Humanities presented an opportunity which might otherwise have failed to materialize until I was too old and too tired to tackle so ambitious a project. The Director of the Youthgrants Program, Glenn Marcus, deserves particular thanks for his sagacious perseverance.

Dr. William Sturtevant, General Editor of the Smithsonian Institution's *Handbook of North American Indians*, assumed a role as this project's tireless advocate. He also read and criticized an almost infinite array of manuscript drafts and provided moral support at crucial moments.

As the project expanded to include a traveling exhibition, the Smithsonian Institution Traveling Exhibition Service (SITES) took on a central role, supporting my work financially and in countless other ways. Among those at SITES to whom I am most grateful are Martha Cappelletti, Exhibition Coordinator, and Peggy Loar, Director.

Felix Lowe, Director of the Smithsonian Institution Press, has expressed a remarkably persistent interest in my work, and my editor, Jeanne Barry, reformed its verbal manifestations with an incisive but light touch. Dick Schmidt and Frank Wiggins were incredibly supportive.

The collections of a great number of repositories were essential to my research. Among those at the Smithsonian Institution were: National Museum of Natural History, National Anthropological Archives (in particular, Paula Fleming); National Museum of American History, Division of Photographic History; and Smithsonian Institution Libraries (in particular, Mary Rosenfeld and Janette Saquet).

Among those repositories outside the Smithsonian Institution were: University of Washington Libraries, Seattle, both the Pacific Northwest Collection and the Historical Photography Collection; also at the University of Washington, the University Archives and Record Center, Edmund S. Meany Papers; the Los Angeles County Museum of Natural History (in particular, Dr. William B. Lee, Director); and the J. Pierpont Morgan Library, New York, Edward S. Curtis Materials.

In addition to Dr. Sturtevant, critical readers of manuscript drafts included: William Stapp, Curator of Photographs at the National Portrait Gallery; William Williams, Professor of Photography at Haverford College; Christine Sherry, attorney and critic-at-large; and Dick Lyman, onetime Professor of History at Stanford University. Due to the limitations in the production schedule and the hardheadedness of the author, not all of their suggestions could be integrated into the final manuscript—they may be credited with its successes, but should not be blamed for its failures. Andrew Murr struggled through the galleys.

Many others ministered to my work and neuroses. Some of these were: Robert Monroe; Manford Magnuson; Lois Flury; Richard Rudisill; Rodney Crowell; Greg Schmidt; Nigel Elmore; the House at 5503 37th Avenue; Laura Greenberg; Dannon Sahara; Laura Brown; Tom Robbins; Fred Strebeigh and Linda Peterson; and many more whose contributions were important but have been omitted from this list in the interest of leaving some room for the text. Last, and anything but least, I would like to thank Alexandra Gleysteen, who survived and then some.

PREFACE

Edward Curtis's belief that he could document "every phase of life among all tribes yet in primitive condition" suggests the immense breadth of his ambition. After studying Curtis's work for years, I am hesitant to fault him for his unbridled aspirations. That he failed to achieve his goals—many of which were founded on illusions—hardly makes his enthusiasm for the attempt seem less laudable. I have found that I disagree with many of his opinions; indeed I have often felt them repugnant. But I have also felt great respect for his willingness to state what he believed. In our attempts to understand cultures different from our own we have often been—and to some extent will probably always be—insensitive. In our future attempts at understanding we may try to be more considerate than we have been in the past, but when no attempts are made there will be no chance for success, however qualified.

As Curtis approached his work in a broad manner, so have I tried to understand it broadly. I have tried to address the simplifications and ambiguities which resulted from Curtis's inability—or lack of willingness—to limit his scope. And in so doing I have introduced some simplifications and ambiguities of my own. I believe that simplification and ambiguity are in themselves neither good nor bad. Sometimes simplification leads to simplistic thinking, yet it may also help us to make use of complex ideas. Sometimes ambiguities are confusing, but they can also keep us from becoming complacent in our understanding of obscure phenomena. In my work, as in Curtis's, judgment as to the legitimacy of simplification or ambiguity rests finally with the beholder.

Even though this book is intended for a general audience, the use of a few peculiar or obscure terms was unavoidable. Anthropometry, for example, refers to the scientific measurement of human bodies. As it is used in this text, aperture means the size of the hole through which light passes into a camera. For most of the terms, a standard English dictionary will be the only reference required. A few, however, are specific to certain times and attitudes. During the period when Curtis was working, anthropology was a developing science. Much of what we now call anthropology was then referred to as *ethnology* (the scientific study of variation among cultures). *Ethnography*, a subset of ethnology, stressed observation over interpretation. Often the line between ethnology and ethnography was blurred by the bias of the ethnographic observer. I have referred to such bias variously as *racism*, *racial prejudice*, or *ethnocentrism*. Simply stated, I have used *ethnocentrism* to describe the confusion of culturally derived beliefs with objective facts. *Racial prejudice* represents an array of ancient fallacies in human thinking, whereas *racism* is a modern concept describing racial prejudice with pejorative connotations. The meanings of *race* and *ethnicity* have often been debated. Now, as throughout their histories, those meanings seem at some times to be obvious, and at others to be utterly impenetrable. I have used the terms *Black*, *White*, and *Indian* to refer to broad groups of people. None of these terms does justice to the individual variation within those groups, and all should be read with skepticism. All are capitalized because—however imperfectly—they describe people.

In *The Vanishing Race and Other Illusions*, I have not presumed to provide definitive answers to the questions I have raised, but rather to contribute to what I hope will be an ongoing discussion of Edward Curtis's work.

C.M.L.

INTRODUCTION

Everyone loves the Edward Curtis Indians. On dormitory walls on various campuses we find noble redmen staring past us into the sepia eternity along with poses of W. C. Fields and Humphrey Bogart. Anthologies about Indians, multiplying faster than the proverbial rabbit, have obligatory Curtis reproductions sandwiched between old cliches about surrender, mother earth, and days of glory. This generation of Americans, busy as previous generations in discovering, savoring, and discarding its image of the American Indian, has been enthusiastic in acquiring Curtis photographs to affirm its identity. Indeed, the many hundreds of thousands of white citizens who have discovered Cherokee blood in their veins since the last census seem to use Curtis pictures to verify the authenticity of their Grey Owl Trading Post buckskin costumes.

How could one set of photographs have this kind of influence? Is it just that we unconsciously connect sepia color and ancient wisdom, as if the browning of America indicated a profound depth of understanding? Or do the poses suggest a vision far beyond any discernible horizon leading us to conjecture with which we have little acquaintance? There are almost as many questions suggested by the Curtis collection as there are photographs. Just when we think we have discovered the secret behind the collection, we are suddenly thrust to new and different insights, and the confusion we initially experienced returns.

The Curtis photographs share a peculiar kind of fate with the famous John Neihardt book *Black Elk Speaks*. Both works are so close to the reality we have been conditioned to see that we assume them to be authentic reproductions of the reality of long ago. Indeed, to suggest that Neihardt did not sit patiently at the feet of the old Lakota medicine man and faithfully take down verbatim his words of wisdom is to place one's life in jeopardy in many places in the Midwest, including a number of Indian reservations. And to remark that Curtis posed his subjects—in some cases provided them with costumes after making them surrender their blue jeans and cowboy shirts—and frequently cropped his pictures to provide a different mood is to reveal one's profound ignorance of the Old West in many an eastern sitting room decorated with Curtis pictures.

When we admit that reality, beauty, and meaning are in the eye of the beholder, we certainly exclude classics, which we have been taught to believe stand above the technical tasks of reproducing the past. Some things, we believe, are above the passage of time and immune to any criticism whatsoever. In this fine work Christopher Lyman strips away these acquired delusions with a rigorous analysis of the photographic art and its technical problems and with a concise but illuminating review of the high points of Edward Curtis's career as a photographer of the western milieu. Lyman does not take a debunker's cynical attitude, chastising Curtis for obvious fakery and romanticism. But rather he provides us with sufficient background so that we can view with a great deal of understanding and some sympathy the gigantic vision that drove Curtis into his major project, *The North American Indian*, at the cost of wealth, health, and family.

Photography in the first decades of this century was partially a useful tool for recording scenes in a West that was rapidly becoming domesticated; it was also a weapon in the final skirmishes of cultural warfare in which the natives of North America could be properly and finally embedded in their place in the cultural evolutionary incline. When one compares the Curtis work with the work of other photographers of his day or of frontier photographers such as John A. Anderson, W. S. Prettyman, A. W. Ericson, and Thomas McKee, the disparity in photographic perception is immediately apparent. These other photographers all seem to present informal scenes of western life—incidents, personalities, and landscapes—that one can confront by simply turning the corner or riding over the next rise. Here, one believes, is history in the making, and if these pictures are stolidly posed, it is because the photographer happened to come upon the scene, quickly set up his equipment, and with little more than a cheerful "Watch the birdie!" recorded the event.

One can hardly accord the same immediacy of historical happening to the Curtis photographs. *The Three Chiefs—Piegan*, for example, taken by Curtis in Blackfoot country in 1907, suggests a movie still rather than a historical event. *Slow Bull Taking an Oath Before Battle* is similarly raw material for the anticlimatic scene in a classic western. And the very popular photograph of the Zuni governor, whose eyes reach out to a reality nearly beyond apprehension, is a picture worthy of enlargement for the marquee at Radio City Music Hall. There are, to be certain, Curtis photographs which suggest daily life in Indian villages and pueblos, but the corpus of the works suggests a timeless reality in which nobility, integrity, and wisdom flourish and prosper.

One could call the Curtis pictures a contrived collection in which representation of life becomes secondary to the task of picturing intangibles which permeate human existence. Lyman makes clear to us that the strands of thought that inspired and informed Curtis were indeed subtle and complicated and if viewed outside their historical context would be understood as promoting and enhancing racism and misunderstanding. One must probe very deeply into the recesses of today's psyche to see the subtle tones of racism in the perpetual fascination of white Americans for portraits of Indians. That racism is indeed there and has a dualistic nature, which all things hidden beneath the surface of psychological perceptions seem to acquire. One encounters the substance of nobility and on returning to the commonplace of daily life is a little irritated that things today cannot have the grandeur of yesteryear, when simplicity and profundity shared the same bed.

More important in understanding the Curtis photographs, Lyman informs us, is to understand the nature of photographic art—its use of colors, its ability to transform through light, and its uncanny use of background to suggest meanings that immediate confrontation with landscape and human activity never seem to communicate. In establishing a pictorial milieu in which things hidden can be revealed, Curtis, together with the several assistants who gave him brilliant technical help in development, seems to have few rivals. As Lyman unravels the various techniques used by Curtis to create moods, meanings, and atmospheres, we feel at first betrayed and tricked by the master's hand, and the synthesis of meaning acquired at first glance dissolves into a fragmented collection of perceptions and ideas. But as we come to understand the delicate weaving of technical procedures with the raw materials of the picture, we are able to comprehend the difficult tasks facing a person who would dare to create a reality of his own and substitute it for the less glamorous substance of history.

Curtis died in 1952, forgotten and obviously a man whose time had long since passed. His photographs of Indians remained the interest of very few, partly because the complete set was terribly expensive, more probably because the optimism of the postwar years overwhelmed any efforts to recapture past glories. America was hell-bent on celebrating its world ascendancy, was about to discover a passel of subversives under its beds, and was completely immersed in the good life for which its adult population had made wartime sacrifices. No time or attention, then, was allocated for photographers of the past with a vision attuned to other realities. True, Curtis photographs were frequently used to illustrate the few books and anthologies dealing with Indians that were published in that decade. But the majority of the work was largely unknown, and had anyone suggested it would again become a popular item, skeptics would have giggled hysterically.

The turbulent sixties resurrected Curtis and endowed his work with mystical attributes. Finding discontent on every street corner and a world they never made, the youth of the sixties cast about for symbols that might express a better reality and a more profound grasp of human experience than the rigid set of conventions which their elders had bequeathed to them. The stolid Indians staring from Curtis's pictures expressing their disbelief in the universe in general immediately brought home to the malcontents the social and political disruptions of the last century, and symbolized for many the survival of human values in a universe gone mad with materialistic greed.

Awakening pride in minority heritage—triggered initially by the movements toward power in ghettos, barrios, and reservations, and further emphasized by linkage to the Vietnam War and the ecological pressures of an aroused citizenry—did much to bring Curtis to the fore as a pictorial spokesman for the real American experience. In virtually no time Curtis's works were in heavy demand and obligatory for people in the movement. Since the photographs did not in the slightest degree speak to the reality of the American Indian, either past or present, they became the perfect format for expression of the wistful reservoir of emotions that lay behind the general perception of Indians. If people could not take cocoa and cookies to Dull Knife's fleeing Cheyennes and piously separate themselves from advocates of Manifest Destiny, they could at least mount a Curtis print prominently in their homes and silently proclaim their solidarity with Indians.

This romanticization of Indians was well received by the Indian community itself. Long separated by geographical and cultural differences, Indians were rapidly creating a national image as a distinct minority group which shared all important incidents as a common heritage. Custer jokes were relevant to every tribe even though only three—the Sioux, the Cheyenne, and the Arapaho—had any stake in further depleting the general's reputation. Drawn increasingly together as an ethnic group and away from their traditions as distinct communities with sometimes malevolent feelings toward other tribes, Indians saw in the Curtis pictures an opportunity to universalize the nobility and wisdom suggested there and claim it as a natural, sometimes even a genetic, Indian trait.

Wiser and more experienced Indians detested the fawning over Curtis. They had previously experienced such periods of intense euphoria inspired by the white majority only to find the climate radically shifting and producing substantial hardships when people forgot their pledge of undying guilt toward the nation's first citizens. Thus a weak smile and an uncomfortable shrug was about the only response that Curtis pictures evoked in older Indians, and many tried to indicate, without condemning, that while these pictures certainly hinted at past glories and innate righteousness, they presented such a sanitized view of Indians that many believed them to be harmful to the cause. From personal experience I can testify to the sense of utter futility these pictures are capable of producing when starting to discuss Indian problems with a prominent senator, I found him shoving a book of Curtis pictures over his desk at me with the remark that he "knew a great deal about Indians."

America may be the only society in human history to move from extreme youth to old age without ever experiencing a period of adulthood. During most of this century we have seen emphasis on extreme youth, and our advertisers concentrate on images which suggest that we can purchase perpetual adolescence by becoming loyal consumers of their products—be they cars, records, cigarettes, or deodorant. In more recent times, as we have discovered our institutions deserting us, have learned of our government's capacity to distort truth, and have experienced the insanity of abstract political and economic doctrines dominating our lives, we have suddenly, it seems, become weary of the whole business and now have little enthusiasm for any more involvement with the world. We have aged rapidly, and not too gracefully, and we find only the artifacts of the past capable of providing comfort for us.

The Curtis Indians have come to occupy a particular place in the pantheon of cherished symbols that inform us about our American identity. As such they relate less to the reality of Indians than we would like and testify to less precise aspects of the American experience—the history we would have liked to have possessed. In this sense they will no doubt always be popular and represent in the public's mind a West and a people that subsequent yearning for certainty has created. If we can learn to view them as photographic art, as the genius of a particular person's efforts to transcend mere photographic recording, then Curtis's work will have made a major contribution to our understanding of the media we use to express our perceptions of reality. But if they come to represent an Indian that never was, and color our appraisal of things Indian with romantic shibboleths that shield us from present-day realities, then our use of them is a delusion and a perversion of both Indians and the artful expressions of Curtis.

Lyman concludes that although Curtis "lied" about Indians with his photography, he must be credited with integrity because of his single-minded concentration on the photographer's art and his insistence that photography could reveal things the way they used to be. Perhaps Curtis was less a liar and more an American dreamer, who felt impelled—as we all do—to create a reality for himself in lieu of the substance of observable things. That he was able to do so, and to do so convincingly, is a final testament to his artistic skills and technical expertise, which cannot easily be surpassed. If this genius shines through the myriad images left to us by Curtis, we have every right to applaud his skills as represented in a subject he has created for us—The North American Indian.

THE VANISHING RACE AND OTHER ILLUSIONS

In the interest of simplicity, diacritical marks have been removed
from titles of images.
Numbers in brackets refer to illustrations.

THE CRITICAL QUESTION:
WHAT IS *THE INDIAN?*

Few photographers have been as dedicated to their imagery as Edward S. Curtis. His multivolume work *The North American Indian* absorbed more than thirty years of his life and an immeasurable amount of his energy. Although the popularity of its more than two thousand images has fluctuated, these images stand as a landmark in the history of artistic photography and as a focal point in the development of prevailing concepts of "the Indian." Neither Curtis's overwhelming devotion to his work nor the artistic power of what he created presents sufficient reason, however, to accept his claim to documentation of a "vanishing race." The composite image of "the Indian" that Curtis bequeathed us was a product of his consciousness and was designed to appeal to the consciousness of his audience. The meaning of that image in the present depends upon our ability to understand the complex factors which influenced its creation. "The Indian," in short, exists only in the mind of the beholder.

Curtis wrote of the painter George Catlin, his predecessor in the depiction of Indians: *He did a remarkable work, one for which the world will always be his debtor. He made mistakes, many of them natural, and anyone working as he did would, perhaps, have made as many. Unfortunately he seems to have had his readers too much in mind and yielded to a desire to interest. In the few cases in which it has been necessary to state a fact that apparently disproves his conclusions, it has been done not in a spirit of faultfinding, but because the situation demands it.*[1]

While Curtis explained that he did not intend to criticize Catlin, my purpose is precisely to criticize Curtis, as he said, "not in a spirit of faultfinding, but because the situation demands it."

Emerging a decade ago from forty years of relative obscurity, Curtis's images have become among the most sought after of American "historical" photographs. A complete set of *The North American Indian* recently sold for $73,000, more than twenty-four times its original price. Ann Horton, of Sotheby Parke Bernet, a major auction house, explains Curtis's preeminence in the photography market as being a result of the breadth of his popular appeal. If pictorial photographs go out of vogue, Curtis's images sell as anthropological documents. If anthropological documents are not in fashion, his images still appeal to fans of pictorialism and devotees of popular imagery of American Indians.[2] Even those who cannot afford to buy original photographs and photogravures can choose from a remarkable array of reproductions of Curtis's work; in posters, books, portfolios, slides, and magazines.

Curtis's tremendous recent popularity is partly a result of changed attitudes about his medium and partly based on attitudes about photography that have not changed. The idea that photography can be used for artistic expression has, after approximately one hundred forty years of debate, finally come into its own. Photographs are hung in the most prestigious museums and galleries, and a master of fine arts degree is granted in photography at art schools around the country. Yet we still look to reproductions of photographs in newspapers, magazines, and books to inform us about the world as it was and is. The applause, in recognition of photography's potential to impart information, which greeted the medium upon its invention in 1839 has not yet faded away, and the original belief that the medium could preserve and present actual reality has maintained a peculiarly strong grip on our imaginations. When we look at photographs made in 1900 or taken on the other side of the globe, we may not necessarily believe that they tell us *the* truth, but we are often still impressed by how they make things and events at such distance of time and space seem so close. Even in an environment saturated with photographic images, photographs continue to impress us in a way which we feel is different from other media, either visual or verbal.

Curtis's popularity is also largely the result of the particular way he used and presented the medium. Calling photography an "art-science," he persistently refused to confine his images within a definition as either one or the other. As is suggested by the

18

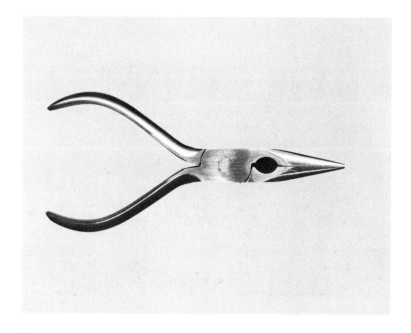

[1] STAHL'S CHAIN NOSE PLIERS, $2.49, 1955
Walker Evans

Edward Curtis called photography an "art-science." Had Curtis chosen
hand tools as his subject matter—as did Walker Evans—the question of
whether his photographs were art or documents might have seemed an
academic argument. Because Curtis photographed people of cultures very
different from his own, it is important to ask how his interest in art
affected his images as documents.

diversity of interests to which his work continues to appeal,
Curtis's attempted fusion of art and science has yet to be seriously examined.

Had Curtis devoted his energies to making photographs of hand
tools—like Walker Evans's photographs for *Fortune* magazine during the 1950s—questioning whether his images were art or documentation might seem an academic argument. [1] But Curtis's
subjects were people. In the 1980s, as we try desperately to
overcome the searing history of racism, there is an urgent need to
understand the relationship between art and documentation in

Curtis's work. If we say that his pictures are art, we imply that
they are Curtis's subjective expression of his reactions to his
subjects. But when we say that his pictures are documents, we
imply that they are objective representations of what his subjects
were. Assuming that racial prejudice is a form of subjective bigotry, it could, in terms of a simple dichotomy between art and
documents, be conveyed by art, but not by documents. The
difference, however, between art and documents, like the difference between racial prejudice and the recognition of cultural difference, is not that simple. Nor can we always identify defini-
tively either of these distinctions.

Edward Curtis was born and grew up in the midst of White
expansion into the American West. In 1868, the year of Curtis's
birth, General Philip Sheridan of the U.S. Army initiated a campaign to subdue Indians on the Great Plains. This campaign was
supposedly aimed only at "warriors," but its victims included a
great many who had made clear their desire to lead a peaceful
existence. Although General Sheridan never specifically endorsed
the killing of unarmed Indians, neither did he object when it
became clear that such was the result of the policies which he had
instituted.[3]

The attitude which Sheridan's campaign embodied was as old
as the history of White settlement of the American continent. It
had taken various forms over some three hundred fifty years, and
had been justified according to a variety of explanations. But
throughout, when the interests of Whites had conflicted with
those of Indians, Indians had usually ended up being killed.

During Curtis's childhood, the mass killing of Indians continued. Despite occasional outcry—usually from those far removed
from the slaughter—the massacre of Indians occurred frequently
and with increasingly ruthless technical efficiency until the killing,
in 1890, of as many as three hundred Dakota at Wounded Knee,
South Dakota.[4] [2] The crime of those killed was their "Indianness," and the punishment was justified under the doctrine of
Manifest Destiny. According to this convenient and often murderous doctrine, those who were thought to be racially "inferior"—
especially Indians—had to be swept from the path of Anglo-Saxon
and Teutonic "progress." If they could be neither enslaved nor
assimilated then the common practice was to exterminate them.

By the turn of the century, White conquest of the continent had
been accomplished, and the tragedy of what had been done in the

name of progress began slowly to dawn upon the populace. Unfortunately, the horror of that recognition was usually distorted by guilt, and instead of being recognized as one of its causes, prejudiced ideas about "race" became a supposed justification for the violence. Even those Whites who shuddered at memories of Indians being killed generally believed that the extermination of Indians was the inevitable outcome of Manifest Destiny.

It was in this context that Edward Curtis set out to construct what he conceived of as a photographic monument to a "vanishing race." Whereas earlier generations had explained their racial prejudice in terms of religion, Curtis's generation believed that it was a legitimate aspect of science or "natural history." If, however, science made clear why Indians had to die, it was also thought that science must preserve what Indians had been like for the benefit of future generations. Much as primatologists have recently attempted to record the behavior of chimpanzees as these animals seem to teeter on the brink of extinction, so had ethnologists of the late nineteenth century applied their observations to what they thought was a vanishing race.

Although we habitually think of anthropology in the present day as objective observation and analysis, it has grown out of a history which included both racial and ethnic bias (or ethnocentrism) among its most conspicuous characteristics. A product of traditional White beliefs, anthropology has reflected some of the most disturbing aspects of those beliefs as well as some of the most virtuous.

As ethnographers set out to make visual records of the "Indian life" which they imagined was disappearing, the camera—which they still believed "never lied"—suggested itself as the ideal instrument. By the time Curtis first began to photograph Indians, they had already been the subject of ethnographic photography for several decades. [3] Like many ethnographic photographers before him, Curtis started out making photographs for other purposes. Some ten years of work had already awarded him a reputation as a popular photographer of romantic portraits and landscapes by the time he decided to make photography of Indians his life's endeavor.

When Curtis embarked upon the project that was eventually to become *The North American Indian*, he took with him both the experiences of having grown up during westward expansion and of having devoted himself almost religiously to exploring the crea-

[2] GATHERING UP THE DEAD AT THE BATTLE OF WOUNDED KNEE, 1891
Photographer unknown

During Curtis's childhood, as in the previous 350 years, the "differentness" of Indians was often perceived as a justification for their extermination. Because Indians were generally believed to be inferior, most Whites thought it was their "manifest destiny" to do away with them in the name of progress.

tion of aesthetic illusion in photography. The images which Curtis made, partly in the name of "science" and partly in the name of art, often exhibited his racial prejudice and ethnocentrism. But to say that prejudice and ethnocentrism were his alone would be a facile mistake.

Just as it was difficult for Curtis to see Indians for what they were through the veil of his culture at the time, so is it difficult for us to see him and his work for what *they* were through the bias of our time. Roughly stated, Curtis's generation believed that Indians were only real Indians when they behaved as they were

imagined to have behaved prior to contact with Whites. Scientists of his generation therefore studied Indians largely in those terms. These general beliefs led to the creation and perpetuation of stereotypes of "Indianness" still prevalent in American culture.

Our generation also seems afflicted with an inverse of this. We are inclined to see Whites as always having behaved the way they behave now. When we describe someone in 1900 as a racist, we tend to think of that person in the terms of a generation which came of age during a spreading of beliefs in civil rights. Even the term racism, however, did not come into common use until well into the twentieth century.[5] Although most Whites believed in the legitimacy of hierarchies according to what they called race, they saw such hierarchies as merely an aspect of taxonomy, and therefore felt no need for a term to describe them. We may use the word racism fairly to describe attitudes at the turn of the century, but only with the recognition that we are imposing a retrospective understanding on a time in which that understanding did not yet exist.

Just as Curtis slipped into thinking in terms of simplistic stereotypes, we too are vulnerable. We are vulnerable not only to the stereotypes of racism but also to those of chronology. Although at the turn of the century most Whites believed in the validity of what we think of as racism, some did not, and there were as many variations in belief in between as there were people to believe them. Use of the term White to describe people of European origins—like the term Indian—lumps together a broad array of ethnic and individual backgrounds. Both terms are expedient and should be viewed with some skepticism. In looking across time, as in looking across variations in skin color, or other less arbitrary characteristics, generalization may be legitimate where

[3] KEOKUK
Daguerreotype by Thomas Easterly
Photographically copied by A. Zeno Shindler
Original before 1848

In the nineteenth century the public believed that photographs showed reality objectively. As a result they thought that photography could preserve what many people were beginning to think was a "vanishing race."

stereotype is not. The line between the two is hard to draw, and to some extent, each of us draws it differently.

In the wake of the civil rights movement of the sixties and seventies we have become at least somewhat conditioned to recognizing the influence of racism in historical literature. Only recently have we begun to see and analyze it in visual documents. We are beginning to understand that although their language and their syntax are different, photographers can manipulate the truth as easily as writers. And they have been equally prone to the influence of racism.

In *The North American Indian*, Curtis presented his images in combination with text and captions. Individually, photographs and words each have meaning of their own. When they are combined, however, their meaning is synergistic—greater than, or at least different from, the sum of the parts. Although much of the text of *The North American Indian* was written by Curtis's assistants, he reviewed their writing and passed judgment on its use with his photographs. Since Curtis chose to present both together, that is also how they can now be most fully understood.

Recognition of the influence of racial or ethnic prejudice upon Curtis's work challenges its importance neither as documentation nor as art. Curtis's contemporaries in a group of photographers called the Photo-Secession were greatly concerned with the establishment of photography as an art, and particularly as an indigenously *American* art. Many of them had traveled to Europe to study art, and all were heavily influenced by emerging European aesthetics, though they did not always choose to admit it. [4] Largely self-educated, Edward Curtis read about art, including European art, with a consuming passion. But the literature and imagery of the American "frontier" exerted a greater influence. Although frontier art and literature were often based as much on mythology as on unbiased observation, that mythology has been an integral part of the development of American culture. By choosing to specialize in rather mythical imagery of "the Indian," Curtis presented an allegory which appealed strongly to a sense of Americanness. [5] Without belittling either their intentions or their products, the Photo-Secessionists never came closer than Curtis came to achieving an indigenously American approach to photographic imagery.

As documents, Curtis's photographs are no less important. His images frequently failed to portray Indians as they actually were.

[4] SELF PORTRAIT
Eduard Steichen

Many of Curtis's contemporaries in the artistic movement known as the Photo-Secession had been strongly influenced by avant-garde European art. They were, however, very concerned with establishing an "American" aesthetic.

[5] A BLACKFOOT
Edward Curtis

Curtis was also very concerned with
aesthetics. His aesthetic was in some ways
more indigenously American than the
aesthetics of the Photo-Secessionists.

But while documents—as a species of fact—are not always true to their intention, they are usually true to something. Curtis's photographs, in conjunction with their text and captions, truly document "the" North American "Indian." Charles Darwin, a thinker in whose intellectual wake Curtis worked, wrote three years after Curtis was born that

false facts are highly injurious to the progress of science, for they often endure long; but false views, if supported by some evidence, do little harm, for every one takes a salutary pleasure in proving their falseness and when it is done, one path towards error is closed and the road to truth is often at the same time opened.[6]

"The Indian," in general, and more specifically *The North American Indian* exist only in the mind of the beholder. That view is supported by evidence from the history of photography; the history of imagery of "the Indian," both scientific and popular; and the history of Indians and Indian cultures. Generalizations from this evidence run the risk, themselves, of lapsing into stereotype and should be judged accordingly.

THE EMERGENCE OF PHOTOGRAPHY AND THE MOVEMENT TOWARD PHOTOGRAPHIC ART

Photography was invented in 1839 during the booming technological development of the middle nineteenth century. It was seen generally as having caused a cataclysmic change in the making of visual documents. Photography's chemical-mechanical process was popularly perceived to have eliminated the subjectivity of human intervention which had been increasingly acknowledged in painting and other prephotographic processes. Photographs, it was thought, presented *things-as-they-were*.

The boom in technological development in the nineteenth-century world has accelerated the rate of change, both social and physical. Praised in the name of progress, awesome in the newness of the things it created, technology was also feared for its capacity to do away forever with much of what was familiar and comfortable in the world. In the face of such fear, it is perhaps understandable that observers were so quick to believe that photography could preserve the world as it had been. The objectivity which was claimed for photography appeared to redeem technology. Technology itself seemed to present the means to protect from its own maw that which it was about to destroy. As technology continued to accelerate change, the public developed increasing motivation for the belief that photography produced objective documents.

Having stunned the public with its presentation of familiar objects close to home, the glass eye of the camera was soon turned outward. As early as the 1840s and '50s, explorers from Europe and America had begun to carry photography to distant corners of the world. When they returned, they brought with them images of far-off and exotic subjects, titillating the curiosity of their less-adventuresome audience, and suggesting that with sufficient diligence, photographers could document the world in its entirety. It was thought that while sitting at home in the comfort of one's own armchair, one could gain through photographs the experience of a world traveler.

From its earliest days, however, this photographic armchair adventure relied on the sensational for its impact. Among the most sensational aspects of the expanding European and American consciousness of the world were the conflicts which developed as empires grew. By 1855, during the Crimean War, British photographer Roger Fenton and others were recording battlefields.[7]

By the outbreak of the American Civil War, photography had so permeated the world's consciousness that it seemed natural to find photographers on the scene, ready to perform their function as documentarists and executors for the armchair adventurer. At the initial battle at Bull Run, Mathew Brady was present and making photographs. Brady had established a reputation as portraitist to the rich and famous of American society and with a romanticism typical of the beginning of the war, conceived it to be his patriotic duty to make photographs of the battles as they occurred. He also no doubt hoped to augment his growing fortune by selling his images of the war to those who had stayed at home in the North. Toward this end he invested a huge amount of capital in assembling a corps of photographers outfitted to follow the war wherever it went.[8]

Like many others, Brady underestimated the devastation a war of such relative technological sophistication would bring about. The photographs made by his camera corps did not sell, and by the end of the war Brady had been financially ruined. The same horror which probably inhibited the public from buying Brady's images only gave further weight to the idea that photographs presented reality itself—even in its bloodiest detail.[9]

Ironically, Brady's camera corps had been unable to photograph anything approximating the bloodiest details of the war. The wet-plate collodion process they employed required too long an exposure to make photographs of the action of battle so they were therefore relegated to depicting the aftermath. [6] It seems that the corps felt the need to dramatize what they did show, as corpses appear posed for effect—in some images blood seems to have flowed uphill and rifles are propped at precarious angles.

Following the war, the government was free once again to direct its attention toward exploring and developing the West. The survey expeditions it funded used photographic techniques, and even some of the photographers, from Brady's camera corps. [7]

Photographers were ostensibly hired for the purpose of providing scientific documentation of their survey expedition's findings. Yet, in both their official work and in the stereocard photographs they made for popular sale, the survey photographers often sacrificed this documentary function to the interest of aesthetic appeal and entertainment. Concentrating on the most sensational aspects of the terrain, they presented striking images of the enormous edifices of the western mountains, of the strangeness of glacial and volcanic geological formations, and of novel forms of vegetation. [8–9]

Among the western survey photographs, perhaps the most exotic to eastern audiences were those of Indians. Western photography had, almost from its inception, turned frequently to Indians as subject matter. In the 1870s, as the scientific focus of the surveys broadened, the newly emerging science of ethnology became an increasingly important element. Photographs of Indians proliferated, but the photographers were not always primarily

[6] SCENE SHOWING DESERTED CAMP AND
WOUNDED SOLDIER
Mathew Brady

Photography was thought to be able to bring distant realities close to home. Photographers, however, often chose sensational subject matter so as not to bore their viewers. Distant wars often satisfied early photographers' search for the sensational.

[7] U.S. Engineering Department Geological Exploration of the Fortieth Parallel
Timothy O'Sullivan

Following the Civil War, the American West became an important source of sensational photographic imagery. Many of the photographers who made images of the West in this period had been trained in expeditionary photography during the Civil War. Among them was Timothy O'Sullivan.

120. CASTELLATED ROCKS ... MONUMENT PARK.

interested in the accuracy of their images as ethnographic documents. Anthropologist Margaret Blackman describes photographs taken by John K. Hillers on the surveys led by John Wesley Powell, noting that many

were taken with a stereo camera and mounted on cards for viewing through parlor stereoscopes, evidence that entertainment value governed the selection of subject matter. The bare-breasted ''Wu-nav-ai gathering seeds'' certainly was not viewed by Victorian gentlemen for its documentation of Great Basin seed gathering.[10] [10]

Photographs made on the western surveys fell short of objective ethnographic documentation not only in the selection of subject matter but also in the posing of subjects and the use of props. It is unclear whether these manipulations were motivated by a desire to appeal to an audience, or the state of ethnographic science was such that they simply did not appear as manipulations to the photographers who used them. Powell, later the founder of the Bureau of American Ethnology, had costumes made for his Ute and Paiute subjects to wear while posing for Hillers's camera—including feather bonnets which may have seemed ''Indian'' to Powell but probably bore no relation to the subjects' normal clothing.[11] That Powell believed in the ethnographic legitimacy of these costumes is indicated by the fact that he sent at least some of them to the Smithsonian Institution to be included in its collections.

Photographers working for the government were not the only ones to photograph the West nor to emphasize the sensational in doing so. They were somewhat constrained—however minimally it may seem to us now—by developing concepts of the importance of objectivity in science. Commercial photographers were under no such constraints.

[8] CASTELLATED ROCKS NEAR MONUMENT PARK
William Henry Jackson

Although photographers working for government surveys of the West were hired to produce scientific documents, they frequently focused on the sensational. They also often sacrificed documentary accuracy for artistic appeal. William Henry Jackson's photographs have long been noted for their artistic strength.

[9] WHITE MOUNTAIN HOT SPRINGS—GROUP OF UPPER BASINS
William Henry Jackson

By the latter nineteenth century, photographs were becoming popularly available as stereocards or in forms of photomechanical reproduction such as this "Albertype." Because photographers emphasized the aesthetically appealing and the sensational, western photographs reinforced romantic illusions about the West among the eastern public.

[10] WU-NAV-AI GATHERING SEEDS
John K. Hillers

Indians were among the more popular subjects for early photographers of the West. Even government photographers such as Hillers made images that appealed to popular stereotypes of "Indianness" and titillated inhibited Victorian viewers. Like Hillers, they often posed and costumed their subjects for effect.

Eadweard Muybridge, a photographer from San Francisco, was skilled in the creation of subtle photographic illusions. Like some photographers of his period, Muybridge "sandwiched" negatives. Using several negatives to make one print, he was able to combine disparate elements into one coherent image. While the use of this "sandwiching" technique was usually limited to the addition of a dramatic sky to a landscape, Muybridge sometimes created such improbable images as a field of rocks which seemed to issue bursts of clouds from its crevices.[12]

In 1873 a group of Modoc Indians took a stand against the United States Army in the lava beds near Mount Lassen in northern California. This affair was of great popular interest in San Francisco, and Muybridge sensed that there might be a market for images of the conflict. Having traveled to the lava beds, he found that he was unable to get close enough to the besieged Indians to photograph them. Instead, he posed Warm Springs Indians, who were working as guides for the U.S. Army, aiming rifles amongst the gnarled rock. Returning to San Francisco, he sold these theatrical images as documents of the "Modoc War."[13] [11]

In his manipulation of his subjects and of the photographic process, Muybridge was typical of photographers of the West. For example, photographers hired by the railroads were paid to make the West look attractive to potential settlers or to eastern businessmen, who might provide further financial backing.[14] Government photographers, as we have seen, often aestheticized their subject matter. They, like the railroad photographers, had employers who were interested in—among other things—the advertising potential of their images. Since the surveys were dependent upon Congress for funding, photographs made by the survey photographers were sometimes given to important senators and congressmen in hopes of encouraging their support.[15]

Taken as a whole, nineteenth-century photography of the West presented an aesthetic vision whose power was an important factor in the process of westward expansion. The splendid West as presented in photographs was a frontier stripped of the commonplace. It was the Garden of Eden which many wanted to believe existed, a magnificent panorama of "views" seldom marred by the mundanities of everyday life. [12] For those who were tired of their lives in the East or were looking for a place to invest their fortunes, this photographic frontier must have seemed irresistibly attractive.

[11] A MODOC BRAVE ON THE WARPATH
Eadweard Muybridge

This image was presented in 1873 as a document of the Modoc Indians, who were fighting to protect themselves against the U.S. Army. In fact it is a portrait of one of the Warm Springs Indians who were working as guides for the army.

For the vast majority of Americans who remained in the population centers of the Northeast, the West existed in images alone. Portrayed as a wild environment, the West seemed filled with drama and populated by Indians whose "savagery" was either noble and picturesque, or in its hostility, seemed a terrific test of the hardiness of White manhood. Dime novels created similar

illusions in which a tendency toward magnificent exaggeration was often recognized, and artists' paintings depicted scenes which were often admittedly fanciful. Had these been the only images available, the myth of the West might have been viewed with skepticism by eastern audiences. Photographs, which had been described as the products of an inherently objective pencil of nature,[16] lent, however, an insidious plausibility to the myth. They were viewed not as metaphors for experience but rather as sections of reality itself. If photographs of the West were exotic, it was assumed that the West must be exotic. If they showed gigantic trees and awe-inspiring mountains, then all the trees were gigantic and all the mountains awe-inspiring. When photographs depicted Indians as "savages," Indians were confirmed as savages in the minds of their eastern audiences.

During the nineteenth century the inherent objectivity of the photographic medium remained largely unquestioned. Its use for documentation was often affected by the subjectivities of its users, but this was seldom noticed and almost never analyzed. When it was noticed at all, the influence of the photographer's subjectivity was usually explained as being a result of the *medium's* inherent mysteriousness—as if photography were beyond human manipulation.

As the nineteenth century drew to a close, however, a slow process of erosion began to gnaw at the belief in photography's inherent objectivity. Photography and indeed technology were becoming omnipresent and therefore less mysterious. The development of photographic technology, in fact, played a profound role in changing both the way photography was used and how its use was viewed.

During the era of collodion photography, between about 1852 and 1880, groups of amateur photographers had sporadically appeared. They were, when judged retrospectively from the era of instant photography, a remarkable example of patience and tenacity. Because the technique required their carting huge loads of cumbersome equipment to whatever scene was to be photographed, the arduousness of their efforts was sufficient to keep the number of amateur photographers relatively small. This arduousness was due primarily to the necessity of exposing glass plate collodion negatives while their emulsions were still wet—if the emulsions were allowed to dry, they became almost entirely insensitive to light. The plates had therefore to be prepared and processed at the scene, and in order to do this, the photographer

was required to carry the entire darkroom apparatus everywhere he went.

Manufacturers of photographic supplies had, by the 1870s, begun to recognize the potential to make a profit from sales to amateurs. No doubt they also recognized that to the extent they were able to simplify the photographic process, their market would grow to include those whose dedication fell short of the complexities of collodion photography. Toward this end manufacturers began to experiment with ways to make a photographic emulsion retain its sensitivity to light even after it had dried.

The manufacture of so-called dry plates had begun by 1880. The products, however, were far from perfect. They were extremely expensive relative to collodion plates, less sensitive to light, and quality control was virtually absent from their manufacture. Dry plates were not an immediate commercial success.

It was George Eastman, owner of a small business in Rochester, New York, who fulfilled the potential of the dry plate. Eastman invented a mechanical method of coating glass plates with an emulsion which lessened their expense and produced a much more consistent product. Although Eastman's company did suffer from technical problems in the early manufacture of dry plates, it adopted a policy of replacing defective materials and strove to perfect its products.[17] By the mid-1880s, the dry plate had almost completely replaced the collodion wet plate, and Eastman's commercial manufacturing process had done away with much of the technical drudgery which had limited the ranks of amateur photographers to a small number.

The expansion of photography that followed the perfection of the dry plate was tremendous, and its effect on the medium was profound. Where the presence of an amateur photographer in a town had seemed remarkable a couple of decades earlier, it began to appear that soon every town would have its own *organization* of photographers. Clubs of amateur photographers sprung up and spread across the country. Their members traded technical dis-

coveries and wrote newsletters about their activities. The newsletters grew into substantial publications, which discussed innovations in the photographic process and, to an increasing extent, the aesthetic potential of the medium.

The proliferation of amateur photography changed the popular view of the medium. Amateurs, unlike professional photographers, were not constrained by the need to sell their work and therefore found much greater freedom to experiment with the medium aesthetically. In the words of a contemporary observer:

Let me say behind a respectful parenthesis that most of the improvements in modern photography have been discovered by amateurs. Working only for pleasure and attainment, the amateur thinks nothing of a risk. He indulges in most unorthodox measures, violating recognized rules of procedure, and with bewildering impunity. Then, the photographer blunders. To blunder is to discover. . . . With his client waiting without to learn the result of the sitting, the professional cannot afford to discover at this price.[18]

The invention of roll film at the end of the nineteenth century brought with it the surrender of the last holdouts against technical drudgery. The introduction of Eastman's Kodak in 1888 made it possible for the casual photographer to make one hundred exposures without reloading the camera.

A short focal length lens, of fixed aperture, meant that no focusing control was necessary and objects from a few feet onwards were sharply rendered. No viewfinder was provided, the camera simply being pointed at the subjects and the 60 degree field of view of the lens allowed a considerable leeway. . . . When the last exposure had been made, the camera was packed up and shipped to Eastman's factory, where it was unloaded, charged with a fresh film and returned. The exposed film was developed and printed and returned to the customer in about ten days. The most revolutionary part of Eastman's system was not the camera, but the concept of separating the operation of taking the pictures from that of developing and printing.

[12] Western Landscape Pictorial
      Photographer unknown

Taken as a whole, photography of the West created a dramatic and often romantic image that must have encouraged the participants in westward expansion.

[13] ARAPAHO SUN DANCE, 1891
James Mooney
Kodak Brownie photograph

Simplification of the photographic process made photography available to amateurs. By the turn of the century, Eastman's Kodak and Brownie cameras had reduced photography from a terribly complex process to the simple clicking of the shutter. Whereas the medium had previously been denigrated as simple and mechanical, comparison with the Brownie began to show that more complex photographic processes required great artistry.

Eastman advertised his camera under the slogan:

PHOTOGRAPHY REDUCED TO THREE MOTIONS. 1. Pull the Cord. 2. Turn the Key. 3. Press the Button. And so on for 100 Pictures.[19] [13]

In addition to making aesthetic experimentation more common, the emergence of nonprofessional photography had another, somewhat ironic effect on the medium and on consideration of its relationship to art. The ease with which photography produced an image seemed conspicuous relative to the mastery required in painting at the time of the medium's invention. As a result, photography had been looked down upon by painters as a simple, mechanistic medium. Supporters of this condescending view pointed to the drab images that were often created as photographic portraiture proliferated among those of only marginal competence, and claimed that they were proof of the debased nature of the medium.

The invention of snapshot photography changed the frame of reference in which photography was viewed. In comparison with the Kodak and its successors, what had once seemed simple and mechanistic, now seemed extremely complex and demanding. The aura of mastery which had once protected painting from the encroachment of photography was beginning to accrue to those photographers who continued to use more elaborate processes.

By itself, however, the introduction of a standard of mastery was not sufficient to make photography acceptable as art. In 1886 Peter Henry Emerson published a manifesto entitled "Photography, A Pictorial Art" which caused a great deal of disturbance in its conclusion that

. . . the modern school of painting and photography are at one; their aims are similar, their principles are rational, and they link one into the other, and will in time, I feel confident, walk hand in hand, the two survivals of the fittest.[20]

The debate as to whether photography could be art rambled on through the 1880s without approaching a resolution. In 1889 Emerson expanded his ideas in his book *Naturalistic Photography for Students of Art*. In the face of continuing adverse reaction, however, Emerson renounced his support of photography-as-art in 1891.

The momentum that had started to gather around photographic art fluctuated, but continued to grow. The theoreticians of established art dug in their heels for a fight, but in so doing they acknowledged for the first time in earnest that there was something to fight about. Conservatives railed against admission of photography to the traditional schools of academic art, pointing again to the repetitive offensiveness of commercial photographic portraiture as evidence that photography was trivial and mechanistic. Photographers tended to behave in an equally defensive manner. Instead of pointing to the aesthetics that had arisen over half a century of unconscious practice in the medium, they aspired to the standards of painting. They retouched, softened focus, and chose allegorical subject matter, but however hard the photographers tried, a painter with a brush still made better *"paintings"* than any photographer with a camera. The failure of photography to match paintings by using the standards of painting only lent further weight to the claims that photography was mechanistic.

The turn of the century was generally a period of upheaval in the arts. Since the mid-nineteenth century at least, artists practicing in diverse media had been exploring visual techniques outside the mainstream of artistic tradition. Objects were depicted within the rectangular "frame" of an image in novel ways, often intersecting each other or the frame's edges. Such placement of objects created an appearance of greater randomness which stressed the subjective viewpoint of the artist over an imagined ideal of visual arrangement.[21]

This tendency toward the admission of subjectivity in vision had been developing for centuries, but had generally been relegated to the margins of established art. By the beginning of the twentieth century such personal vision had left the margins and begun to encroach upon the artistic mainstream. It was over this mainstream of established art that the conservative academics presided, so that they were often jealous in the protection of their domain. For centuries they had worked to maintain traditions in art and to inculcate their students with those traditions. The academics perhaps understood that the movement toward subjective vision threatened those standards—that if the movement became generally accepted, they would lose the prerogative of passing judgment as to the legitimacy of artistic endeavor.

In their adherence to traditional standards, however, the academics had become vulnerable to accusations of artistic stagnation. Their judgments about artistic legitimacy began to appear more as prohibitions than as accreditations. By the end of the nineteenth century academic art had fallen into a nostalgic sentimentality the conservatism of which was coming to be seen increasingly as an inhibition to creativity.

In the challenge that began to be mounted against the restrictions of academic art, photography played a central role. The belief that photography produced objective visual documents had been trumpeted as relief for painters and engravers from the mundane tasks of reportage. Lady Elizabeth Eastlake, writing in 1857, had suggested that artists could leave the primacy of concern for subject matter to photographers and devote their attention more exclusively to aesthetic concerns.[22] Photography, bearing out this suggestion, had helped to catalyze the conceptual separation in other media of form from subject matter, thus paving the way for aesthetic abstraction.

At the same time that it was being touted for its objectivity, photography was becoming an aesthetic force in its own right. The general reticence to *call* photography art had clearly done little to inhibit its use in an aesthetic manner; that it was *not* called art meant that its aesthetic use had not been circumscribed by the strictures of academic standards.

Thus photography, the estranged cousin of the visual arts, took over much of the responsibility for aesthetic innovation. That estrangement, however, which allowed photography to function as a vehicle for aesthetic experimentation, also precluded acknowledgement of its effects on other media. When artists in the late nineteenth century looked at photographs, it is questionable how aware they were of aesthetic mediation by the photographers. Still, the more artists confused photographs with reality, the more they allowed photographic aesthetics to enter their perception of reality, and therefore to influence their art.

Before photography could itself become acceptable as art, it had to overcome the popular belief that it was solely the product of machines and of nature, and to prove that it allowed human intervention. Having failed to achieve this end through the limitation of painting, many photographers had become frustrated. By the turn of the century they were becoming bolder, and in their frustration, some photographers turned to a form of visual polemic. Attacking photographic conventions, they scratched negatives, scribbled on prints with crayons, and generally attempted to force their audience into recognition of their involvement in the making of the image. Other photographers refused to engage in

[14] A SNAPSHOT; PARIS (1911)
Alfred Stieglitz

In 1903 Alfred Stieglitz founded a group of photographers called the Photo-Secession, which was dedicated to the advocacy of photographic art. Stieglitz believed that photographers should not try to imitate painting but should recognize photography's own aesthetics. He worked in the relatively unmanipulative school referred to as "straight photography."

such behavior, insisting that photography had already proved its aesthetic potential—that its aesthetics differed from those of other media, but were no less profound.

Among the most articulate and influential of turn-of-the-century proponents of art photography was Alfred Stieglitz. Stieglitz had studied photography in Germany under the famous pioneer of photographic optics, Dr. Herman Vogel. In Europe, Stieglitz had been subjected to the antiacademic attitudes of emerging artistic salons and had become convinced that photography could be a legitimate medium for the creation of visual art.[23]

Over the most active years of Stieglitz's career, between 1885 and 1930, his attitudes about art and photography changed a great deal. Volatile in temperament, Stieglitz was prone to acerbic rhetoric in support of whatever was his current interest. But his commitments to photography-as-art and to its advocacy among at least the avant-garde of the art world were profound. Stieglitz marked the emergence of art photography as having occurred during the 1890s, saying in 1899 in an essay for *Scribner's Magazine* that

before that time pictorial photography, as the term was then understood, was looked upon as the bastard of science and art, hampered and held back by the one, denied and ridiculed by the other. It must not be thought from this statement that no really artistic photographic work had been done, for that would be a misconception; but the point is that though some excellent pictures had been produced previously, there was no organized movement recognized as such.[24]

Stieglitz went on in the essay to attack the conception of photography as a mechanistic medium. Admitting that the medium had often been used mechanistically, he implied that this use was caused by the economic necessity among commercial photographers of producing a volume of work. The medium itself, Stieglitz indicated, was neutral, and in this respect did not differ from other media in the visual arts. He quoted P. H. Emerson:

The painter learns his technique in order to speak, and he considers painting a mental process. So with photography, speaking artistically of it, it is a very severe mental process, and taxes the artist's energies even after he has mastered technique. The point is, *what you have to say and how to say it*. The originality of a work of art refers to the originality of the thing expressed and the way it is expressed, whether it be in poetry, photography, or painting.[25]

Stieglitz became progressively more convinced that in order for "pictorial photography" to attain acceptance as art, it would have to prove that its performance accorded with the "highest"—if not the most traditional—of aesthetic standards. At first Stieglitz pursued the establishment of such standards in the framework of existing clubs for amateur photographers, eschewing what he saw as the crass commercialization of professional photography. For several years he used his position as editor of the house organ for the Camera Club of New York, *Camera Notes,* to express his views and those of others who sympathized with him. The membership of the club, however, did not often share these views, and in 1902 Stieglitz resigned his position to found a group for those who shared his avant-garde ideas. The Photo-Secession, as Stieglitz called the group, was dedicated to proving by example that photography could produce art of the highest order.[26]

Stieglitz was convinced that what he called "the masses" were reactionary in spirit, and that only through the efforts of an elite of "so-called extremists" would they be compelled to recognize the artistic potential of photography. Intending the Photo-Secession to become just such an elite, Stieglitz wrote that

its aim is loosely to hold together those Americans devoted to pictorial photography in their endeavor to compel its recognition, not as the handmaiden of art, but as a distinctive medium of individual expression. The attitude of its members is one of rebellion against the insincere attitude of the unbeliever, of the Philistine, and largely of exhibition authorities.[27]

Toward these ends Stieglitz opened a gallery, known as "291" for its address on Fifth Avenue, and published an expensively produced journal called *Camera Work.* A luxurious forum, *Camera Work* was illustrated by extremely fine photogravure reproductions, the printing of which was supervised by Stieglitz. However, during the period in which the journal was published it never reached more than a small number of patrons.

Stieglitz was himself a proponent of what came to be known as "straight photography"—that school which asserted that photography had its own pure aesthetics which should not be diluted by extensive manipulations of its process. [14] Among the Photo-Secessionists, however, Stieglitz tolerated the often manipulative styles of Eduard Steichen and Gertrude Käsebier, and even the visual polemics of Frank Eugene. [15] Although he often spoke to

[15] THE POOL
Eduard Steichen

Other photographers, even among the Photo-Secessionists, were more manipulative in their creation of artistic pictorials. Some, such as Eduard Steichen, continued to be strongly influenced by painting.

the contrary, Stieglitz's criteria, it appears, had less to do with technique than with the attitudes of the artists and their faithfulness to the elevation of photographic art.

Viewed in retrospect the Photo-Secession was not so revolutionary in what it *did* with photography as in what it *recognized* in the medium. It was, in effect, a consolidation of radical viewpoints and imagery with an insistence that photography owed art no apology. The elitism of the Stieglitz approach made the Photo-Secessionists' work and ideas inaccessible, both economically and conceptually, to "the masses." Stieglitz believed, however, that the general public could not comprehend what the Photo-Secessionists were trying to say, and therefore were not an important audience (though he professed to appreciate what he saw as their lack of pretension).

Although never specifically defined as such, the real task of the Photo-Secessionists was to convince their audience to give up their belief in the inherent objectivity of photography. They chose to limit that audience—in their own time, at least—to those who were already receptive to persuasion. In so doing the Photo-Secessionists ensured their success, and that success, in turn, insulated them from the general public who most needed persuading.

Even among the Photo-Secessionists and their patrons, assertion of the *potential* for subjective expression through photography did not dictate the view that all photography was necessarily subjective. Although consumingly concerned with the potential for subjective expression in photography, the Photo-Secessionists did not destroy the pervasive belief that photography could freeze things-as-they-were, thereby saving them from the ravages of time and change. They did lay much of the conceptual groundwork for the construction over succeeding decades of a distinction between photography as art and photography as documentation.

GETTING INTO
GOOD SOCIETY

Edward S. Curtis was born in Wisconsin in 1868 on what was still the frontier of westward expansion. When Curtis was a boy, his family moved to Cordova, a village in rural Minnesota.[28] Only a decade before, the pioneers of Minnesota had been engaged in a bloody struggle with the Santee Sioux, nine-tenths of whose lands they had seized.[29]

Curtis's career as a photographer grew out of a boyhood hobby. In his teens he worked as an assistant in a photography studio in St. Paul. Then, shortly after the family's move in 1887 to Seattle, Washington, Curtis's father died, forcing Curtis to abandon his photographic career in order to support the family. In 1891 it reemerged when, mortgaging part of his homestead for capital, he bought into a partnership in a photography studio with Rasmus Rothi. This was superseded in 1893 by a second partnership with Thomas H. Guptill.[30] On December 14, 1896, a Seattle magazine, the *Argus*, heralded the Curtis and Guptill Studio as "one of the greatest examples of business energy and perseverance to be found in Seattle today. . . ." The same article noted "the award of a bronze medal to Curtis and Guptill for excellency in posing, lighting and tone at the convention of the Photographer's Association of America."[31]

Having parted with Guptill in 1897, Curtis continued in business as Edward S. Curtis, Photographer and Photo-Engraver. Apart from photoengraving, his stock-in-trade consisted primarily of portraits and romantic pictorial views of scenery from the Northwest. [16]

In 1898 Curtis combined these interests in what was to become the focal work of his life—photography of Indians. Indians were, in the minds of most Whites at the time, neither entirely human nor entirely unhuman. They were thought to be human enough for a photograph of an Indian to be considered a "portrait"; at the same time, however, they were thought to be part of "nature" (in a way in which Whites were not) and therefore part of the local scenery. An interviewer for the *Hampton Magazine* explained

that "he wished to touch nature with his camera, and the Indians of the Northwest were ready to his hand."[32]

Curtis's new specialty was promoted by a chance meeting, also in 1898. As described by his daughter, Florence Graybill, Curtis was climbing Mount Rainier when he encountered a party in distress. The group included C. Hart Merriam, chief of the U.S. Biological Survey, Gifford Pinchot, chief of the U.S. Forestry Department, and George Bird Grinnell, popular ethnologist and editor of *Forest and Stream* magazine. Curtis befriended these eastern dignitaries by rescuing them. The friendship proved extremely helpful, for the following year Grinnell asked Curtis to join the E. H. Harriman Expedition to Alaska.[33]

E. H. Harriman was an enormously wealthy financier and industrialist from New York. The expedition had originally been intended as a family outing for the Harrimans, but it turned into a lavishly financed variation on the earlier federally-funded surveys of the West. Perhaps less pragmatic than the western surveys in its emphasis on such academic disciplines as ornithology and entomology, the expedition included thirty natural scientists whose mission it was to describe and chart the resources of Alaska.

In addition to Grinnell, Pinchot, and Merriam, such prominent figures of the time as naturalists John Muir, John Burroughs, and Louis Agassiz Fuertes joined the journey north. [17] The expedition also included geologists, foresters, botanists, zoologists, and taxonomists. These eminent men were provided with a library of five hundred books relating to Alaska, and they delivered nightly lectures in the main cabin of the steamship *George W. Elder,* which had been chartered for the trip.[34]

The expedition generated some five thousand photographs, many of which were made by Curtis and his assistant. Interestingly, of the photographs reproduced in the ten volume publication covering the expedition, those credited to Curtis were almost exclusively of landscapes and geological formations. [18–19] The

[16] MOUNT RAINIER
Edward Curtis

Edward Curtis was a moderate in the argument as to whether photographs could be art. His images, however, were highly artistic, and he began to achieve a nationwide reputation as a photographic artist by the mid-1890s. Although he was mainly a photographer of studio portraits and landscapes, Curtis began by 1898 to make artistic photographs of Indians around his native Seattle.

ethnographic images of Alaskan Natives in these volumes were mostly credited to C. Hart Merriam.

During the years leading up to the Harriman Expedition, Curtis had become something of a local hero in the Seattle area. He was the city's most respected professional photographer, winning awards for his work at the national level. After his return from Alaska, Curtis's national exposure increased. He began, with considerable encouragement from the regional photographic press, to act as an emissary from the West to the world of art photography.

Curtis was not as certain of the relationship between photography and art as Alfred Stieglitz was, nor was he so strident in his attempts to gain recognition for the aesthetic potential of his medium. Stieglitz's extensive education and his exposure to the latest artistic trends in both the United States and Europe had given him a self-confidence that was often arrogant. Curtis had begun his photographic career as a student of a book on photographic processes, *Wilson's Photographics: A Series of Lessons Accompanied by Notes on All the Processes Which Are Needful in the Art of Photography*.[35] He had very little formal education and had never been abroad. His knowledge of photography had come from years of the kind of practical experience which Stieglitz looked down upon as crass commercialism, and from a consuming curiosity which had driven him to read whatever was available on the subjects of art and art history. Curtis's confidence as an authority on art photography was that of a self-taught scholar, and he sometimes showed signs of defensiveness.

Writing a column on amateur photography in a Seattle magazine called the *Western Trail*, Curtis noted in 1900 that "many artists claim that a photograph cannot be a work of art." He then deferred to the "artists'" judgment:

I do not think the most radical of them can deny that a photograph can show artistic handling and feeling. After all, it is the finished picture that hangs upon our wall, and not the implements with which it is made.[36]

Like Stieglitz, Curtis believed that in their efforts to elevate photographic aesthetics, photographers had to transcend mere imitations of painting. He saw the medium, however, in terms of a fusion of art and science, which Stieglitz had denigrated as an outmoded bastardization.

When I say that we should study for a greater art education I do not mean that we should try to make our work like a brush or a pencil artist.

[17] MUIR AND BURROUGHS
Edward Curtis

In 1899 Curtis was selected as the official photographer on an expedition to Alaska funded by Wall Street magnate E. H. Harriman. The expedition included many prominent scientists of the period, such as John Muir and John Burroughs. The prestige of having been selected as official photographer strengthened Curtis's reputation.

Photography is one of the greatest art sciences and is able to stand for itself. Let us study light and shade, composition and perspective, both as it is seen in nature and in the work of the masters, not to copy but to learn. Once we know the true rules of art it will soon be shown in our work.[37]

Curtis recognized the importance of subjective expression as a criterion for photographic art.

Try to make your work show some individuality, or in other words, make it look yourself; let it show that you have put part of your life into it.[38]

He cautioned his readers, however, not to carry their personal vision too far. "Do not seek to astonish," he wrote, "but to

[18] ISLETS IN SITKA HARBOR

[19] SUN AND CLOUDS

    Edward Curtis

Most of Curtis's photographs from the Harriman Expedition depicted landscapes and geological formations. Among these photographs were some examples of his skill as a romantic pictorialist.

[19]

please." When describing those whose aim it was to astonish their audience Curtis's mildness of manner disappeared:

People are making stuff they call new-school photography, which they and their worshippers marvel at for the most unsensible, blind reason that they can't understand it. . . . It is so impressionistic that one don't [*sic*] know what to make of it, and the only impression a sane man receives is that rather more than the usual possible number of mistakes happened . . . that the unlucky devil who did all this tommy-rot has somehow got into good society before he was taught the way to behave. . . .[39]

Curtis's advice to amateur photographers that they should seek "to please" was reflected in his own work. During the year 1900, several of Curtis's images were published as halftones in *Camera Craft*, the leading journal of photography on the West coast. *Camera Craft* was much closer to the photographic mainstream of the time than was the still nascent Photo-Secessionist journal *Camera Work*. Whereas *Camera Work* presented itself as a forum for the elite of the avant-garde, *Camera Craft* strove to present and to analyze a broad array of contemporary work. Although *Camera Work* has come to occupy a more prominent position in our consciousness of the history of photographic aesthetics, *Camera Craft* was read in its own time by a greater audience and probably had more immediate impact on attitudes about photography.

Curtis was among the most respected of the photographers whose artistic work was published in *Camera Craft*. *Why?*, published as a supplement to the October 1900 issue, was a sentimental example of Curtis's early style of portraiture, as was the untitled Aristo Print published the following year. [20–21] These images displayed the concern for lighting and posing from which much of Curtis's popularity had arisen. They also appealed to the sometimes maudlin tastes which pervaded academic art of the period. These images, however, referred more to Curtis's past than they did to what was becoming the central theme of his life's work.

Although Curtis was not responsible for the ethnographic photographs which resulted from the Harriman Expedition, his experience during the voyage must have stimulated his developing interest in ethnographic subject matter. Upon return from the expedition, George Bird Grinnell convinced Curtis to accompany him on a trip to Montana to photograph Indians on the Blackfoot

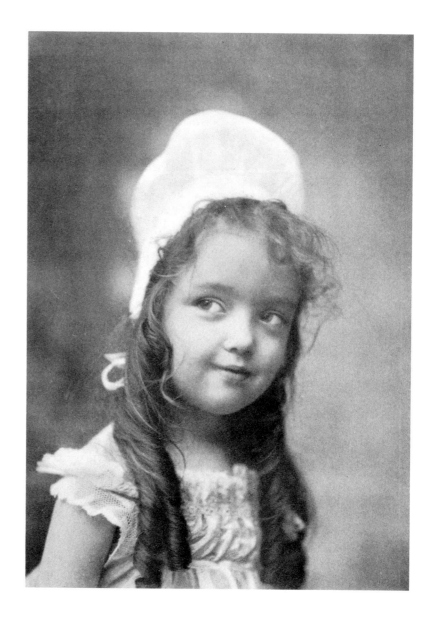

[20] W H Y ?
Edward Curtis

Edward Curtis's studio portraits had drawn attention to his mastery of posing and lighting in the creation of pictorial effect.

[21] Aristo Print
Edward Curtis

Although Curtis was of humble origins, his sophistication in photographic
aesthetics had attracted a clientele from among the wealthy and powerful.

Reservation. Grinnell, an avid popularizer of ethnography, had
himself experimented with photographing Indians, but was far
from expert with the medium. Having recognized the appeal that
aesthetically pleasing photographs would bring to his field, Grinnell encouraged Curtis to pursue photography of Indians full time.

In the fall of 1900, at about the same time that Curtis and
Grinnell were heading for the Blackfoot Reservation, *Camera
Craft* published an article on the Twentieth Annual Convention of
the Photographers' Association of America:

Starting with the address of President Stein, who drew attention to the
fact that the followers of art photography are traveling over the same
ground that the painters have already traversed from the excessive detail
of the pre-Raphaelites, who painted Nature as she is, "and not as she
looks to be," . . . to the extremes of the impressionist school, in which
detail and lines were lost beyond recognition, and lastly to a sane middle
ground in which the greatest modern painters are working. So photographers have passed from F/64 [a very small lens aperture which renders
detail in extreme definition] to fuzzywuzzyism, and thence to a better,
truer, and more balanced position.[40]

On the same page, as an example of this "more balanced position," is a halftone reproduction of a Curtis photograph, *Evening
on the Sound*, and on the facing page another, entitled *The Clam
Digger*. [22–23] These photographs—which drew first prize in the
"genre class" at the convention—are actually different framings
of the same scene. The sand being dug in *The Clam Digger*
appears again just to the left of the canoe's bow in *Evening on the
Sound*. The subjects of these images are presumably Indians. Due
to their backlighting (which, given Curtis's emphasis on lighting,
was indubitably a conscious choice) they appear as silhouettes,
and their "Indianness" is only implied by the canoe. Interestingly, however, both images appear again thirteen years later in
the portfolio of gravures accompanying volume nine of *The North
American Indian*.

Neither of these images as they appeared in *Camera Craft*
made any claims as ethnographic documents. They were romantic
pictorials, which incidentally included Indians as subject matter,
and they were presented as such. They were indicative, nevertheless, of the direction in which Curtis's work was headed.

Also suggestive of Curtis's new-found interest in ethnography
was another pair of images published in *Camera Craft* later the
same year. *A Desert Queen* and *The Egyptian* were published

[22] EVENING ON THE SOUND

[23] THE CLAM DIGGER

Edward Curtis

Among the most famous of Curtis's early pictorials were those he made of Indians in 1898. They were not intended as ethnographic documents, but rather as artistic images appealing to popular romantic stereotypes of ''Indianness.''

[23]

without accompanying text to explain the pointed suggestion that the sitters were exotically ethnic. *A Desert Queen* depicts a Black woman in a loose-fitting, low-cut garment which gave the appearance of being no more than a piece of fabric serving as an adaptable studio costume. [24] The woman is lit softly from above and to the side, lending a romantic air to her questioning pose. The allusion to royal bearing is supported visually by her tiara and necklace of heavy trinkets. It appears that we are to infer that she is from the desert because she wears flowing headgear and because she is Black.

In *The Egyptian* the subject stands in strict profile to the camera, alluding to traditions in ancient Egyptian portraiture and to one of the poses that was standard in anthropometric photography of the period. [25] She wears the same tiara and necklace which appeared in *A Desert Queen*, indicating that these were studio props the ethnicity of which was purely imaginative. Aside from her pose, her studio prop jewelry, and the ornate box on which her right hand is placed, there is nothing in this image to explain the "Egyptianness" of its subject. Backlighting obscures—presumably intentionally—the details of the subject's face. On close inspection it appears that she is not Egyptian at all—rather that she is Caroline McGilvra Burke, wife of a Seattle judge, Thomas Burke, and frequent subject for Curtis's camera.

Far from unusual at the turn of the century, imaginative depictions of ethnicity such as those in *The Egyptian* and *A Desert Queen* were a minor vogue in pictorial photography. For other pictorialists, F. Holland Day and Gertrude Käsebier, for example, ethnicity was a vague and intermittent interest stimulated by the desire to find or create subject matter which was exotic and therefore appealing to their audience. [26]

Curtis may originally have been moved by similar motivations. By 1900, however, he had become convinced of the importance of specialization, as is evident in the advice he offered readers of his column in the *Western Trail*. "Let me urge you to make a specialty of some one thing. This is a day of concentration, and to make a showing you must be a specialist."[41] Guided by his own advice, Curtis was receptive to George Bird Grinnell's suggestion that he devote himself full time to photography of Indians.

[24] A DESERT QUEEN
Edward Curtis

Following his exposure to ethnographers on the Harriman Expedition, Curtis began to become increasingly interested in ethnic subjects. This studio portrait created the illusion of ethnicity by using studio props, costumes, and a Black sitter.

[25] THE EGYPTIAN
Edward Curtis

The sitter for this studio image is probably not Egyptian. She appears to be Caroline McGilvra Burke, the wife of a Seattle judge and frequent poser for Curtis's camera. She is depicted wearing some of the same studio prop jewelry as appears in *A Desert Queen*.

[26] Untitled Portrait of Indians Accompanying Buffalo Bill's Wild West Show
Gertrude Käsebier

Edward Curtis was one of many pictorialists who used ethnic subjects or allusions to ethnicity to create an air of the exotic in their works. For other pictorialists, however, ethnic subjects were a passing fancy.

Barbarians and Savages

Specialization such as that which Curtis advocated in 1900 was very different from that of modern academic disciplines. It is not unusual to find modern anthropologists who specialize in such narrow areas of the field as ethnobotany or economic anthropology or, more recently, visual anthropology, and whose training includes a decade of study within one discipline. But in 1900 anthropology was still a fledgling science. Many of its practitioners had no extensive academic training in any field, much less in anthropology or a specialty within anthropology. Relative to what had come before, however, Curtis's observation that his was "a day of concentration" was indeed accurate.

Although Europeans had been making unscientific observations of human diversity for centuries, from their first discoveries of cultures different from their own, they had been more impressed by the *otherness* of the people whom they encountered than by any variations among those people. Moreover non-Europeans—or non-Whites—were perceived as having failed to live up to the standards of European culture and of Christianity and were therefore assumed to be inferior. Images of a nonagricultural existence, which included cannibalism, sexual promiscuity, and the general absence of what most Europeans considered to be morality, filtered into European consciousnesses. Offsetting these frightening and distasteful images were reports of a primal intimacy with the physical environment, the lack of political organization, and a general simplicity of life.

But whether perceived as vicious and sinister or as simple and noble, non-Whites were lumped together under such terms denoting inferior otherness as "savage" or "barbarian."

After the discovery and colonization of America, the original inhabitants of the continent—Indians, as they came to be called—became the focus of White concepts of savagery. During the centuries that followed, White imagery of Indians shifted back and forth between viciousness and nobility. Throughout these shifts, however, the preoccupation with Indian "savagery" prevailed to such an extent that the diversity of Indian cultures went virtually unnoticed. No less persistent was the presumption that in their unitary otherness, Indians, even if they were noble, were inferior to Whites.

Over these first three and one-half centuries, most Whites' observations of Indians were incidental byproducts of proximity and were subject to the biases which that proximity often fostered. Among the few to pursue ongoing contact with Indians for abstract reasons, missionaries were so constrained by the belief that they were bringing improvement to the Indians whom they met that they reinforced concepts of Indian inferiority more often than they challenged them. White traders and trappers sometimes transcended cultural barriers by living with and even marrying Indians. But the bridge between cultures could only be crossed in one direction—a White trapper or trader who lived with Indians became a savage himself in the eyes of most other Whites, and his acceptance of Indian cultural values was likely to be viewed with the utmost suspicion.[42]

By the mid-nineteenth century, contact between Whites and Indians was changing drastically. Indians had been removed from the population centers of the East, either by extermination or by forced exodus to reservations or to areas in the West as yet uninhabited by Whites. The westward compression of Indian populations brought diverse cultures into contact and forced greater numbers of people to survive on a fixed availability of resources. Given the circumstances, it is surprising how little friction resulted among the tribes which had been thrown together. But when friction did result, it was seen by Whites as further evidence of Indian savagery.

As Whites began to encroach on the last areas of Indian domain, the idea that Indians were a race destined to disappear began to gain currency. It was at approximately the same time that emerging concepts of "natural science" began to be extended to the study of human behavior. Whereas the presence of Indians had generally been seen as a menace, the idea of their disappearance gave rise to a nostalgia that was often cloaked in the trappings of science.

Theories of biological evolution and attempts at biological classification had proliferated throughout the late eighteenth and early nineteenth centuries. These classifications and theories were extremely varied, and there was no general agreement on any one as an explanation or description of biological phenomena. This began to change in 1859 when Charles Darwin published his theory of natural selection in *The Origin of Species*.

Darwin himself was less concerned with perceived racial variations among humans than he was with abstract questions about biological evolution. About racial diversity, he wrote that

. . . all races agree in so many unimportant details of structure and in so many mental peculiarities that these can be accounted for only by inheritance from a common progenitor; and a progenitor thus characterised would probably deserve to rank as man.[43]

Darwin was not, however, beyond suggesting that in non-White peoples a model might be found for an earlier stage in the evolution that had led to Whites parroting the prevailing European ethnocentrism of the preceding centuries. He stated that

. . . there can hardly be a doubt that we are descended from barbarians. The astonishment which I felt on first seeing a party of Fuegians on a wild and broken shore will never be forgotten by me, for the reflection at once rushed into my mind—such were our ancestors. . . . He who has seen a savage in his native land will not feel much shame, if forced to acknowledge that the blood of some more humble creature flows in his veins. For my own part I would as soon be descended from that heroic little monkey, who braved his dreaded enemy in order to save the life of his keeper . . . as from a savage who delights to torture his enemies, offers up bloody sacrifices, practices infanticide without remorse, treats his wives like slaves, knows no decency, and is haunted by the grossest superstitions.[44]

As science became increasingly concerned with human variation, it assumed many of the bigotries and vast generalizations which had preceded it. The vagueness of such value-laden terms as ''savage'' and ''barbarian'' began to give way to ''scientific'' classifications according to race. Such classifications often proposed or presupposed the hierarchical ranking of humans, and although the categories and systems of classification were only slightly less vague than those which they replaced, they were supposed to have been derived from rational analysis of empirical observations. Thus science, under the theory of survival of the fittest, seemed to confirm the legitimacy of racism. As Thomas Gossett has described:

The nineteenth century was obsessed with the idea that it was race which explained the character of peoples. The notion that traits of temperament and intelligence are inborn in races and only superficially changed by environment or education was enough to blind the dominant whites. The Indians suffered more than any other ethnic minority from the cruel dicta of racism. . . . In general, the frontiersmen either looked forward with pleasure to the extinction of the Indians or at least were indifferent to it. The intellectuals were most often equally convinced with the frontiersmen that the Indians, because of their inherent nature, must ultimately

disappear. They were frequently willing to sigh philosophically over the fate of the Indians, but this was an empty gesture.[45]

It was in this intellectual environment that the science of anthropology emerged. Military campaigns of extermination were still being carried out against Indians in the West, utilizing sophisticated weaponry with the most deadly effect, and being justified under the ideological banner of Manifest Destiny. According to that doctrine, White Anglo-Saxons were preordained by virtue of their innate superiority to dominate inferior races so as to gain access to the land and resources. The government surveys of the West—on which ethnology was confirmed among the ranks of the sciences—had been organized for the express purpose of cataloging those lands and resources still under Indian domain.

The ethnological researches by Henry Rowe Schoolcraft and Lewis Henry Morgan which preceded the western surveys had been pursued because of abstract curiosity about and feelings of affinity for Indians. While these reasons were certainly the primary motivations among government ethnographers as well, the ethnographers were not beyond justifying their funding from Congress in terms of the usefulness of their researches as military intelligence.[46] Although the implication of ethnology's significance as military intelligence was doubtlessly a concession to economic expediency, government ethnology incorporated in all seriousness a great deal of racist ideology.

John Wesley Powell was deservedly considered among the most enlightened White observers of Indians in his time. He nevertheless saw fit to publish an article by C. C. Royce in the *First Annual Report of the Bureau of American Ethnology* entitled ''Investigations Relating to the Cessions of Lands by Indian Tribes to the United States'' in which Royce justified cessions of Indian lands.

The great boon to the savage tribes of this country . . . has been the presence of civilization, which, under the laws of acculturation, has irresistibly improved their culture by substituting new and civilized for old and savage arts, new for old customs—in short, transforming savage into civilized life. The great body of the Indians of North America have passed through stages of culture in the last hundred years achieved by our Anglo-Saxon ancestors only by the slow course of events through a thousand years.[47]

Without specifically mentioning Manifest Destiny or evolution, this justification strongly implies the hierarchical frame of reference in which intellectuals of the period viewed cultural variation. By referring in abstract terms to their own culture as "civilization," and to the interactions between their culture and Indian cultures as "acculturation," White scientists obscured their subjective bias behind a veil of jargon. But beneath the jargon, the message bears striking similarities to the ethnocentrism which preceded the nineteenth century's fascination with "scientific" description. Anglo-Saxon "civilization" (the "new") was still seen as superior, and Indian "savagery" (the "old") as inferior.

Despite the adherence to traditionally hierarchical distinctions between cultures, the point of view expressed in this article was—for its time—mildly progressive because it opposed the belief that inferiority was a racial characteristic which was biologically determined, and that there was no hope ever for Indian "improvement."

In this article, while Indian "savagery" was seen as a primitive step in an evolutionary path culminating in Anglo-Saxon "civilization," nevertheless, it was implied that "under the laws of acculturation," Indians had improved. This analysis now seems highly ironic: an "irresistible improvement" which included the death of thousands of people hardly seems a "great boon."

It is difficult in retrospect to unravel the tangle of conditions and motivations which led to the emergence of scientific study of culture. As an example of early ethnology, the article by Royce is somewhat misleading. Ethnologists attempted only infrequently to apply their researches to the changes in cultures around them. Instead, they focused on recording and understanding cultures they believed to be on the brink of disappearance. A fear of loss much like that which had fostered a belief in the objectivity of photographs encouraged the public to believe that with sufficient diligence, science could preserve whatever was valuable in cultures that were disappearing.

Ethnologists generally saw Indians as innately inferior. The tendency to see that perceived inferiority in Darwinian terms as a primitive stage of evolution nonetheless made Indians seem intellectually useful as models of that from which Whites had evolved. Thus while most ethnologists shared the belief that "improvement" of Indians through acculturation—the acceptance, that is, of White culture—was a positive development, they also believed that there was *something* in "Indianness" that was worth preserving. Unfortunately, the use of Indians as evolutionary models,

however stimulating to turn-of-the-century researchers, was to distort the pursuit of anthropological science for almost a century.

Under the ethnocentric assumption that the emergence of European cultures marked the pinnacle of human evolution, nineteenth-century Whites speculated about explanations for the difference between their culture and others. Some believed that Indians had evolved along lines similar to those of European cultures, but had regressed to a level of "savagery." Others believed that Indians, by virtue of their supposed biological inferiority, simply evolved more slowly than Whites. Ethnologists and ethnographers tended toward the latter view and incorporated it as a central premise in formulating their approach to the study of Indian cultures.

Within the internal logic of their ethnocentrism, early ethnologists theorized that change in Indian cultures was so slow as to be imperceptible. That Indian cultures *had* changed since contact with Whites was an obvious fact. The threat that this fact posed to the concept of Indians as unchanging was blithely explained away in this manner:

Indians had changed since contact with Whites because of something—apparently due to innate White superiority—that made them acculturate or accept aspects of White culture.

To the extent that they acculturated, Indians lost that vague quality of "Indianness," in effect became less "Indian."

Thus when Indians changed, they were no longer Indians, and the fallacy that Indian culture did not change remained sacrosanct.

It was from this circular reasoning that the concept of the "ethnographic present" emerged, and although it has not always been applied consciously, it remains a defining characteristic of historical ethnology. Under the concept of the ethnographic present, Indians were studied in the context of the time when their ethnicity was thought to have last existed in a "pure" form. In the early days of ethnology, this generally meant that researchers attempted to study Indian cultures in terms of what they were—actually what they were *imagined* to have been—prior to contact with Whites. There was a kernel of legitimacy to be found in this concept: insofar as one was interested in cultures because they were *different* from one's own, it stood to reason that as a culture became more *like* one's own, it also became a less interesting object of study.

As the study of culture developed into modern anthropology, it changed, though often subtly and with little recognition of the reasons for changing. The emergence of academic anthropology in the early twentieth century under the influence of Franz Boas constituted a movement away from traditional ethnocentrism. Boas, who as a professor at Columbia University trained most of a generation of American anthropologists, taught that cultures should be studied as much as possible within their own terms. Although he and his students did a great deal to mitigate the imposition of White values on the study of Indian cultures, they nevertheless left the concept of the ethnographic present largely intact.

As early as the 1890s, ethnologists such as James Mooney, who worked with the Bureau of American Ethnology, had begun to study the effects of acculturation. Although acculturation research did bring the study of culture into a more dynamic and contemporary frame of reference, it was far from representative of the bulk of anthropological investigation. The Meriam report on the contemporary status of Indians in American culture, commissioned by the Institute for Government Research and published in 1928,[48] and the program of applied anthropology, instituted by Commissioner John Collier of the Bureau of Indian Affairs during the 1930s, pushed the study of anthropology further toward the "actual" present, as did Margaret Mead's innovative efforts with the study of contemporary culture. In spite of these developments, however, some anthropologists still continue to describe non-White cultures as "primitive."

The branding of cultures in recent times as primitive is not racism in the sense in which theories of racial hierarchy were consciously applied in the late nineteenth and early twentieth centuries. Rather, this phenomenon seems to be the result of an uncritical acceptance by some anthropologists of traditions whose roots are far removed in time.

Curtis Focuses

In 1899, when Edward Curtis was first being exposed to professional ethnography as a member of the Harriman Expedition, James Mooney had only recently completed his first acculturation studies. Lewis Meriam would not publish his report for the Institute for Government Research, *The Problem of Indian Administration,* for another thirty years. The term racism had not yet been coined, and among many Whites, ethnologists included, "race" was seen as a legitimate indicator of biological tendencies in behavior. Anthropology had not yet gained acceptance as a discipline of academic study, and its practitioners, under the titles of ethnologist and ethnographer, had been trained according to a motley array of informal methods. Thus Curtis, with a background in commercial and artistic photography, was not so unlikely a candidate for recognition as an ethnographer.

Shortly after his trip to the Blackfoot Reservation with George Bird Grinnell in 1900, Curtis made his first trip to the Southwest for the purpose of photographing Indians. It is clear that by this time, either through persuasion by Grinnell or through his own volition, Curtis had decided that in his "day of concentration" he would specialize in photography of Indians. He had already received acclaim for his earliest images of Indian subjects, and the "business energy and perseverance" for which he had also been noted no doubt made him sensitive to the popular market for such images. There is no record of the exact point at which Curtis decided to make what he later called "a comprehensive and permanent record of all the important tribes . . . that still retain to a considerable degree their primitive customs and traditions." It appears, rather, that the idea developed gradually over a period of several years and was bolstered by the support, both moral and financial, of friends and colleagues. Moreover, it was during this period that Curtis began a transition, also gradual, and never complete, from commercially oriented art photography to the peculiar fusion of art and ethnography for which he is best known.

In February 1901, *Camera Craft* published an article entitled "A Critical Review of the Salon Pictures with a Few Words upon the Tendency of the Photographers." The article was written by Arnold Genthe, a San Francisco photographer who often worked in a pictorialist aesthetic. Genthe, like Curtis, had experimented with ethnic subjects in a series of photographs taken of San Francisco's Chinatown, and would in 1908 spend six months making photographs in Japan.[49] He also traveled to the Southwest where he photographed Indians in 1898, 1911, and 1926.[50] Of Curtis's photographs taken in 1900, Genthe said:

[27]

[28]

[27] MOTHER AND CHILD

[28] SPECTATORS

Edward Curtis

Following his decision to specialize in photography of Indians, Curtis continued to stress the importance of artistic effect. These two highly retouched images display different presentations of the same negative.

E. S. Curtis' Indian studies occupy quite a place by themselves. They are of immense ethnological value as an excellent record of a dying race, and most of them are really picturesque, showing good composition and interesting light effects. "The Moqui Chief" ["Moqui" was then the usual English name for the people now called Hopi] is a stunning portrait of the haughty Indian, and is, perhaps, even of greater artistic merit than "The Mother" and "The Moqui Girl", both pictures of great human charm. "The Three Chiefs" just misses being great. If the head of the foremost horse could have been turned so as to break the straight line formed by the three horses the composition would have been perfect. But, even as it is, the photograph is a very beautiful rendition of a picturesque phase of Indian life.[51]

Genthe's recognition of the "immense ethnological value" of Curtis's photographs is one of the first indications that they were beginning to be presented as ethnographic documentation rather than solely as pictorialist genre studies. The photographs to which Genthe refers imply that this was a change in presentation, but not a change to any great extent in Curtis's approach to his photography. [27–28] It is to the "artistic merit" of the images that Genthe devotes most of his attention, and his explanation of their ethnographic significance is in vague terms of their "rendition of a picturesque phase of Indian life." [29]

Edward Curtis was, by all accounts, a man of enormous energy and it seems likely that with the same intensity as he had approached the study of photography, he had decided to educate himself about ethnography. But whereas he had been reading about and practicing photography for some fifteen years by the time his photographs began to receive artistic acclaim, Curtis had been studying ethnography for at most two or three years prior to this review by Genthe. Public attention, however, seemed to freeze the basic elements of Curtis's approach to ethnographic photography. During the next thirty years Curtis was to be exposed to a diverse variety of ethnographic viewpoints, but his style fluctuated only mildly. The orientation of his photographs was, at the completion of *The North American Indian,* strikingly similar to that which he developed in these early years.

A Desert Queen and *The Egyptian* were among the last pseudo-ethnographic pictorials which Curtis set up in his Seattle studio. But they were indicative of the manipulations both of his subjects and of virtually every step of the photographic process contrived by Curtis and his assistants in creating a composite image of the "North American Indian."

An article based on an interview with Curtis and published in the *Times* of Seattle on November 15, 1903, reported:

According to Mr. Curtis' own statement he was led into his present habit of flattening the Indian up against a negative through the desire to reach out after a picturesque subject.

Further, the article innocently explained that Curtis's images did not depict Indians as he had found them. It described Curtis's manipulations of his images, not in terms of a threat to their accuracy as ethnographic documents, but rather with admiration for the illusion which has was creating.

Instead of the painted features, the feathers, the arrows and the bow, we find him in [the] blue jeans and cowboy hat of semi-civilization. Enshrined though he may be with the weird habits and mysterious rites of his forefathers, the mystery has vanished and the romance has gone in the actuality of the present day.

And so Edward S. Curtis, of Seattle, found him. For the time being Curtis became an "Indian." He lived "Indian;" he talked it, he was "heap white brother." The best years of his life were spent, like the renegades of old, among the Indians. He dug up tribal customs. He unearthed the fantastic costumes of a bygone time. He won confidences, dispelling distrust. He took the present lowness of today and enshrined it in the romance of the past. . . . he changed the degenerated Indian of today into the fancy-free king of a yesterday that has long since been forgotten in the calendar of time.

He has picked up a bundle of broken straws and erected a palace of accuracy and fact. What Greene has been to the English people Curtis has been to the American redmen.[52]

During the seven years between 1900 and publication of the first volume of *The North American Indian,* Curtis's work concentrated on that which was of greatest popular interest. Although his studio continued with commercial work under the Curtis name, Curtis's photography of Indians was an expensive undertaking which had to support itself financially. Thus, although Curtis's interest in ethnography exerted a growing influence on his work, the salability of his images remained a necessary priority. Perhaps to enhance the commercial appeal of his work, Curtis focused during these early years on those tribes with whom the public were most familiar and whose appearance could most easily be made to conform to popular imagery of "Indianness."

By the turn of the century, the tribes of the Southwest had already become the objects of a thriving tourist trade. The rail-

roads servicing the area played an active role in creating this trade by publishing advertisements illustrated with halftone reproductions from photographs of Indians and Indian "scenes" in popular magazines. Such advertisements presented Indians as an exotic spectacle that was part of the natural landscape of the West, thereby appealing to a nostalgia about cultures which Whites had formerly feared. In 1903 the Atchison Topeka & Santa Fe Railroad published a popular guide entitled, *Indians of the Southwest*. Written by George Dorsey, a respected ethnologist, this text treated southwestern Indian cultures with greater subtlety than much of the literature generated by the tourist trade. Still, it was far from free of ethnocentrism, and, ironically, by stimulating the tourist trade, the guide contributed to the destructive pressures exerted by that trade on the cultures that were its objects.

Perhaps even more than the tribes of the Southwest, the Great Plains tribes occupied a place of prominence in White imagery of "Indianness." Whereas the aesthetic magnificence of the Pueblos and their surrounding landscapes made the tribes of the Southwest easily salable as a tourist attraction, there was little public interest in tourism among the tribes of the Great Plains. On the other hand, the struggles between these tribes and encroaching Whites were a matter of fascination to easterners. Unlike earlier struggles, the conquest of the Great Plains had taken place during an era when the popular press had the means at its disposal to report what had or was imagined to have occurred. Such reports often pandered to White imagery of Indian savagery. Dime novels told stories of White swashbucklers who braved bloodthirsty hordes, and captivity narratives presented stilted tales of supposed Indian barbarity. These publications presented an image of Indianness to an audience which had no direct contact with Indians and was therefore uncritically receptive to the imagery.

Following the cessation of armed conflict on the Great Plains, the public was curious to see the largely fictional Indians it had read about. Plains Indians, as they were living on western reservations, did not in reality conform to popular imagery. Lacking the basis for a tourist trade such as that in the Southwest, the Plains Indians were transported to the East as actors in fantastic "Wild West Shows." These shows were circuslike dramas which glorified White-Indian warfare with sham battles and presented Indians as the bloodthirsty savages whom easterners had read about.

Largely as a result of this widespread contact with fictional characterizations, Whites came to see the image of the Plains Indian as the quintessential representation of Indianness.

It is hardly surprising that Curtis, a commercial photographer whose specialty was imagery of Indians, should have devoted his initial attention to those tribes most familiar to his potential customers. [30–35] Thus his work prior to publication of *The North American Indian* concentrated on the tribes of the Southwest and of the Great Plains.

Still the model of "business energy and perseverance," Curtis sold his images in a wide variety of forms. Prints were available, first on heavily textured paper with a relatively cool hue, and then on smooth paper with a warm reddish hue imbued perhaps by copper toning.* Appealing more explicitly to the tourist trade, Curtis also published a series of postcards of Indian subjects. [36] These halftone reproductions were printed on textured stock and were cropped differently from his photographic prints—the postcards had a ¾-inch white border at the bottom and titles in calligraphy descending vertically down the right side of the image.

_____
* This hue could also have been the result of a variety of other toning processes which were popular during the period.

[29] THE THREE CHIEFS—PIEGAN
Edward Curtis

Curtis won awards for this and other photographs. As his fame continued to increase, he began to be recognized as a photographer of Indians. Another artistic photographer, Arnold Genthe, hailed Curtis's photographs as "of immense ethnological value." Despite being touted for their supposed ethnographic significance, Curtis's images remained oriented toward artistic renditions of popular imagery.

[30]

[30] SHAM BATTLE—INDIAN CONGRESS, 1898
Credited to F. A. Rinehart

Wild West Shows presented dramatizations of supposed Indian behavior that reinforced White stereotypes of "Indianness." Sham battles, such as the one depicted, encouraged the racially prejudiced image of Indians as inherently bloodthirsty. Largely because of the focus of the Wild West Shows on the Great Plains tribes, those tribes became representative of "the typical Indian" in the minds of many viewers.

[31] WILLIE HOLY FROG
Photographer unknown

Many popular photographers of Indians were not as sophisticated as was Curtis in the depiction of stereotypes of "Indianness."

[32] HORN DOG AND FAMILY
[33] CHIEF WILDSHOE AND FAMILY
Photographer unknown

Costumed Indians were often photographed with symbols of White culture. The "humor" of such images traded on racist stereotypes of Indians as primitively inferior.

[34] GOOD MORNING
[35] KAW CLAA—A THLIGET MAIDEN
Case & Draper

Indian women were often presented in ways alluding to stereotypes about their supposed promiscuity. These images did not strike the White public as pornography only because their Indian subjects were generally thought to be less than human.

[31]

[32]

[33]

[34]

[35]

[36] Z U N I W A T E R C A R R I E R S
Edward Curtis

Post cards, such as this one published in 1904, made Curtis's appeal to a popular market explicit.

The subjects of these postcards were primarily from southwestern tribes, but also included some from the Great Plains and from the area around Seattle, where Curtis's reputation had been most firmly established.

In the production of his images for commercial sale, Curtis relied extensively on the staff of his Seattle studio. He developed his own negatives on location and made contact prints from them using the cyanotype process. Cyanotypes, very similar to architectural blueprints, could be produced easily using sunlight for their exposure, making access to a darkroom unnecessary. Having produced this cyanotype "proof," Curtis sent the negative to his studio where prints were made following instructions written by Curtis on the cyanotype.

In 1903 Curtis hired a darkroom assistant with impressive credentials. Adolph F. Muhr had worked previously for Frank A. Rinehart, one of the most famous photographers of Indians at the time. Although Muhr worked as Rinehart's assistant, he actually made a great number of the photographs for which Rinehart was credited and which earned Rinehart his fame.[53] There is, however, no indication that Muhr took any of the photographs of Indians credited to Curtis. It *was* Muhr—referred to as Curtis's "able co-worker"[54]—who performed the manipulations of darkroom process essential to Curtis's imagery. There is no evidence to suggest that Curtis did any of his own laboratory work following the hiring of Muhr. It seems possible, therefore, that Muhr also played some part in the invention of a process variously called "gold-tone," "Orotone," or, after Curtis, "Curt-tone." Of this process—which was not introduced until later in his career—Curtis said:

The ordinary photographic print, however good, lacks depth and transparency, or more strictly speaking, translucency. We all know how beautiful are the stones and pebbles in the limpid brook of the forest where the water absorbs the blue of the sky and the green of the foliage, yet when we take the same iridescent pebbles from the water and dry them they are dull and lifeless, so it is with the orthodox photographic print, but in the Curt-tones all the translucency is retained and they are as full of life and sparkle as an opal.[55]

Curt-tones were in fact glass plate positives backed with imitation gold leaf. Those parts of the image which in a normal print are white are reflective in a Curt-tone, creating an almost mirrorlike effect.

Curtis's commercial use of his images was not limited to the sale of individual prints. Two of his photographs were reproduced in Dorsey's *Indians of the Southwest*. As his reputation as an authority on Indians spread, Curtis began to deliver lectures, using lantern slides made from his photographs as illustrations. He also began to publish illustrated articles in popular magazines, discussing Indians and his work with Indians in terms more candid than was typical of his contributions later to the text of *The North American Indian*.

By 1904 Curtis's ambitions were broadening and the idea for publication of *The North American Indian* was taking more definite shape. During the years he had spent in the Southwest and on the Great Plains, Curtis had also made periodic trips to the East, meeting and discussing his work with ethnologists. Although it is doubtful even then that Curtis thought of himself as an ethnographer in the strictest sense (after he had finished *The North American Indian*, he still deferred to the expertise of others), he believed that his work was of ethnographic significance. Many of the experts with whom he had discussed his photographs had encouraged him, saying that his images were among the best ethnographic records they knew of. In a letter to Fredrick Webb Hodge, then at the Bureau of American Ethnology, and later the general editor of *The North American Indian*, Curtis expressed his growing confidence:

The longer I work at this collection of pictures the more certain I feel of their great value. Of course, in the beginning, I had no thought of making the series large enough to be of any value in the future, but the thing has grown so that now I see its great possibilities, and certainly nothing could be of much greater value. The only question now in my mind is, will I be able to keep at the thing long enough and steady work [*sic*], as doing it in a thorough way is enormously expensive and I am finding it rather difficult to give as much time to the work as I would like.[56]

Financial concerns obviously still haunted Curtis. While the distractions which those concerns presented frustrated him, Curtis was beginning to see that the glowing opinions of ethnologists could be of some assistance in mitigating his financial woes. Curtis was often powerfully idealistic, but in addition to a belief in the importance of ethnographic photography, his idealism included a profound desire to fulfill his sense of himself as an example to all of the self-made man. Even though Curtis described himself as being solely motivated by a desire to "further

the work," the publicity which he arranged frequently focused on him as much as on his work.

Roosevelt, Morgan, and the Immortalization of Edward Curtis

The year 1905 was a particularly active time in Curtis's pursuit of publicity, and one in which his efforts conspicuously paid off. He launched the year with shows in Washington, D.C., first at the Washington Club, then at the Cosmos Club—of which John Wesley Powell (1834–1902), founder of the Bureau of American Ethnology, was a cofounder. With the assistance of C. Hart Merriam and Mr. and Mrs. E. H. Harriman, Curtis was able to obtain an audience with the president of the United States, Theodore Roosevelt.[57] Roosevelt, often noted for his machismo and fondness for the image of the intrepid frontiersman, had in the past expressed a disparaging view of Indians as a "race":

I suppose I should be ashamed to say that I take the Western view of the Indian. I don't go so far as to think that the only good Indians are the dead Indians, but I believe nine out of every ten are, and I shouldn't inquire too closely into the case of the tenth. The most vicious cowboy has more moral principle than the average Indian.[58]

Roosevelt had studied at Columbia University under John W. Burgess in 1880. Burgess was one of the primary architects of the Teutonic Origins Theory, a variation on Manifest Destiny which maintained that those of Teutonic origins were the pinnacle of human evolution. Roosevelt did not adhere to the Teutonic Origins Theory, but it appears that he accepted the more general tenets of "scientific" racism, and he was most certainly a believer in Manifest Destiny.[59]

This belief in Manifest Destiny, however, constituted no barrier to Roosevelt's appreciation of photographs which Curtis described as representing a "vanishing race." In fact, Roosevelt's appreciation of those photographs was so great that he became one of Curtis's most devoted and influential fans. On March 27, 1905, when Curtis opened a show of his work at the Waldorf-Astoria in New York, invitations to the exhibition included a letter from Roosevelt to E. H. Harriman. The letter praised Curtis's images, declaring that "not only are Mr. Curtis's photographs genuine works of art, but they deal with some of the most picturesque phases of the old-time American life that is now passing away."

Curtis apparently spent most of 1905 promoting his work, since few of his images were copyrighted in that year. He did photograph the Roosevelt family for a supplementary portfolio to *McClure's* magazine, and he continued to mount shows of his work in cities throughout the East. Moreover, in June he hired John C. Slater, an advertiser from Seattle, to help with his promotion. As described in an article in the Seattle *Times*:

. . . Mr. Slater will bring universal attention to the enormous value of Mr. Curtis' work and secure for it the appreciation which it deserves. To quote one brief but significant expression by Mr. Slater himself: "These pictures will immortalize Edward Curtis. Ten years from now he will be the most talked of man in the United States in that line of work."[60]

A broadside, presumably published by or at least for Curtis, presented "some letters and extracts regarding Mr. Edward Curtis and his work." Among those quoted were W. H. Holmes, chief of the Bureau of American Ethnology—then part of the Smithsonian Institution—and one of his ethnographers, Matilda Cox Stevenson. Holmes's letter is quoted in reference to Curtis's plan to publish his work. "I sincerely hope that you will succeed in this most commendable undertaking. The series of volumes would be a monument to yourself and especially to the institution making the publication possible." The irony of this statement became apparent when in later years Curtis repeatedly and unsuccessfully tried to convince the Smithsonian Institution to buy a subscription to *The North American Indian*. Although he certainly had his fervent admirers in the Institution, it nevertheless resisted his salesmanship—perhaps because of the skepticism of its secretary, C. D. Walcott—and finally acquired a set as a donation from Mrs. E. H. Harriman.[61]

In December 1905 Curtis returned to Washington, D.C., for another show at the Cosmos Club. During this show, Curtis received a letter from Roosevelt which was perhaps the most important step toward realization of Curtis's plan for *The North American Indian*:

There is no man of great wealth with whom I am on sufficient close terms to warrant my giving a special letter to him, but you are most welcome to use this letter in talking with any man who has any interest in this subject.

After lavishing praise on Curtis's work, Roosevelt concluded the letter with an endorsement of the idea that Indians represent a primitive stage in the evolution of man.

You are doing a service which is much as if you were able suddenly to reproduce in their minute details the lives of the men who lived in Europe in the unpolished stone period. The publication of the proposed volumes and folios, dealing with every phase of Indian life among all tribes yet in primitive condition, would be a monument to American constructive scholarship and research of a value quite unparalleled.[62]

Roosevelt's hesitance to address this letter specifically was perhaps because of fear that his trust-busting activities would make such an address seem presumptuous. Ironically, Curtis probably used the letter when he introduced himself to one of Roosevelt's wealthiest adversaries, J. Pierpont Morgan.[63]

On January 23, 1906, Curtis wrote to Morgan, sending him a proposal for *The North American Indian* in preparation for a personal audience on the following day. In his letter Curtis explained that he could provide "ample endorsement" of the "scientific accuracy" of his work, but encouraged Morgan to judge its "artistic merit" for himself.

In the accompanying proposal Curtis described the format as including

. . . twenty volumes containing fifteen hundred full page plates, the text to treat the subject much as the pictures do, going fully into their history, life and manners, ceremony, legends and mythology, treating it in a rather broad way so that it will be scientifically accurate, yet if possible, interesting reading. . . .

In addition to the book, the plan includes the publication of seven hundred of the more important pictures in the size now on display 14 × 17 to be placed in portfolios containing 35 pictures each. Illustrations, both large and small, to be of the best photogravure work, and both pictures and text on the best paper. Binding and paper to be such that it will be as lasting as paper can be made.

Implying doubt about his own authority as an ethnographic scientist, Curtis explained that

it is presumed that I and my field assistant will collect and compile the text which will later be turned over to men in the scientific field, recognized as authorities, to edit, thus affording unquestionable authenticity.[64]

Curtis was naively optimistic about the magnitude of the project he proposed, predicting that his field work could be completed in five years, when in fact it was to take four times that long. He estimated his field expenses as approximately $15,000 a year, including, among other things, salaries for three assistants; expenses for railroad transportation, livery, and hotel accommodations; and fees for interpreters. Significantly, there was also in this estimation of expenses an entry of $1,450 for "Money paid Indians." Indicating that he had already invested some $25,000 in his work so far, Curtis explained that he intended to continue to rely on the staff of his Seattle studio.

Curtis's request to Morgan was not for an outright grant, but rather for an interest-free capital loan of $75,000 to cover field work for the projected five years. The loan was to be repaid to Morgan in sets of the finished publication. Curtis had originally intended that *The North American Indian* should be published and marketed by a commercial publishing house and that repayment of his loan from Morgan should be taken from his royalties for the work.

Morgan, impressed with Curtis and his work, approved the proposal, and plans for the publication began to be implemented. Attempts to find a commercial publisher were to no avail, as *The North American Indian* required a capital investment larger than even the most prosperous publishing houses were willing to risk. Reluctant to guarantee such an investment against loss, Morgan convinced Curtis to publish and market the work himself.[65] The burden which this put on Curtis, both as a financial drain and as a distraction from his photography, was to plague him for the rest of his life.

During 1906 Curtis directed most of his attention to *The North American Indian*. He completed his field work for the first two volumes on the Southwest and made general preparations for publication. Writing to Fredrick Webb Hodge—the scientific au-

thority who had been chosen as general editor of the series—Curtis was enthusiastic about the progress he was making. He also explained that he had been delayed slightly because the San Francisco earthquake had destroyed some of his photographic equipment.[66]

By the following year, despite delays and distractions, the work on the first volume was complete and *The North American Indian* went to press for the first time.

Theodore Roosevelt was neither an authority on photography nor an authority on ethnographic science. He was, however, a most influential patron, and one whose opinions could be expected to appeal to those who were wealthy enough to afford $3,000 for a set of *The North American Indian*. "In Mr. Curtis," wrote Roosevelt, opening his foreword to the series, "we have both an artist and a trained observer, whose pictures are pictures, not merely photographs; whose work has far more than mere accuracy, because it is truthful."

At a time when the potential for subjective expression in photography was recognized only by a small group of what were considered aesthetic extremists, this statement by Roosevelt would not have disturbed a popular audience. He paid tribute, therefore, to the conception of photography as a mechanistic medium, but implied that Curtis's photographs were different in that they were "pictures." Roosevelt, it seems, was trying to say that Curtis's images were art without offending the many who still believed that photographs *could not be* art. But at the same time he made extravagant claims for their significance as documents which were "far more than merely accurate."

HOW *THE INDIAN* WAS MADE

It was from this attempt at combining art with science that *The North American Indian* had been conceived. In the general introduction to the series, which follows Roosevelt's foreword, Curtis wrote:

Rather than being designed for mere embellishment, the photographs are each an illustration of an Indian character or of some vital phase in his existence. Yet the fact that the Indian and his surroundings lend themselves to artistic treatment has not been lost sight of, for in his country one may treat limitless subjects of an aesthetic character without in any way doing injustice to scientific accuracy or neglecting the homelier phases of aboriginal life.

Curtis continued, appealing to the popular belief that photographs captured "nature" as-it-was and could therefore preserve what was useful and interesting about "the Indian" for posterity:

. . . being directly from Nature, the accompanying pictures show what actually exists or has recently existed (for many of the subjects have already passed forever), not what the artist in his studio may presume the Indian and his surroundings to be.[67]

It is true that Curtis often photographed his subjects where they lived, and to that extent he was not "the artist in his studio." Commercial photographers had frequently made images of Indians against romantic painted backdrops, and compared to such images Curtis's photographs were probably convincing as "being directly from Nature." But they were not, and given Curtis's methods, this claim is revealing of his attitudes toward truth and his conception of reality.

Curtis did not bring Indians to his studio to photograph them, but he did take his studio to the Indians whom he photographed. He carried as part of his standard equipment a studio tent with an adjustable skylight to create whatever lighting effects he desired. He did not use painted backdrops, but he did use a backdrop of maroon muslin (see *Typical Apache*). Had these constituted his

only manipulations, his claim to "show what actually exists" might have remained plausible. In fact, through an elaborate array of techniques, Curtis very actively set about making his images conform to what he believed "the Indian and his surroundings to be."

Curtis's consciousness of photography and of "Indianness" were still very much of the era of his childhood. In keeping with traditions in White thought, Curtis was so affected by his perception of Indian "otherness" that he often overlooked the extreme diversity of the cultures he confronted and described Indians in terms of an imagined racial unity as "the Indian." Curtis clearly recognized that there *were* differences among the tribes and people whom he photographed. These differences, however, appear to have been subsidiary in his mind to a perception of racial character. As Curtis conceived of it and wrote in his general introduction, *The North American Indian* was "a comprehensive and permanent record of all the important tribes . . . that still retain to a considerable degree their primitive customs and traditions." It was also a monument to a "vanishing race," a nostalgic tribute to the composite stereotype of "Indianness" which had dominated White imagery for centuries. "To the workaday man of our own race," wrote Curtis, "the life of the Indian is just as incomprehensible as are the complexities of civilization to the mind of the untutored savage."

It was the "untutored savage" which Curtis intended to present. "Savages" and "primitiveness" were, and had always been, imaginary constructs which could be presented in photographs only through imaginative use of the medium. Assuming that he was not purposefully deceitful, Curtis must have seen his manipulations of his subjects and of the photographic process as adding "truthfulness" to a medium that was inherently "accurate."

The "truthfulness" which Curtis added to his photographs conformed to Whites' imagery of Indian "primitiveness." Indians were generally seen, even by professional ethnographers, as culturally static. If they *did* change, they were no longer Indians. As Roosevelt wrote in his foreword:

The Indian as he has hitherto been is on the point of passing away. His life has been lived under conditions through which our own race past so many ages ago that not a vestige of their memory remains. It would be a veritable calamity if a vivid and truthful record of these conditions were not kept.[68]

Indians and Indian cultures, like other people and other cultures, did and do change. In proximity to White cultures, changes in Indian cultures had tended to incorporate behavior which to Whites seemed un-Indian—in the terms of professional anthropology, Indians had "acculturated." Acculturation had, however, been going on for centuries; the evolutionary predecessor whom Roosevelt described existed only in the minds of Whites. "The Indian as he had hitherto been" was no more than an image.

By the turn of the century conquest of the North American continent was complete. To the extent that this marked a precipitous change for Indians, it was in the loss of yet more control over their lives to cultural imperialism. It is true that more Indians adopted the clothing, forms of housing, and occupations of the cultural mainstream than had ever before been the case. But this was often a matter of survival, not of choice. Indians' cultural identities, though under heavy assault, did not always change with their clothing. The disappearance was of that vague quality in individual Indians which Whites could recognize as "Indianness." Perhaps then, it was guilt about their often dictatorial control of Indians, in addition to centuries of killing and death from their diseases, which led Whites to the illusion that Indians were disappearing.

In his attempts to create an artistic image of "Indianness," Curtis was in fact "doing injustice to scientific accuracy," and "neglecting the homelier phases" of the lives of the people whom he photographed. The injustices to scientific accuracy were not terribly different in kind from those considered common practice among ethnographic photographers of the late nineteenth century. Curtis, like most other ethnographic photographers, saw truthful depiction of Indians as showing only what he believed to be part of their "primitive" Indianness. His conception of primitiveness, although never clearly defined, appears to have been based on the popular illusion that change depleted Indianness—that true

Indianness was that which was unaffected by White culture.

Curtis seems therefore to have believed that by removing evidence of the influence of White culture from his photographs, he *was* being more *truthful* in his depiction of Indians. In this context, the use of a studio tent might have seemed justified because it could exclude all but intended subject matter. Outside the studio tent, the problem of excluding subject matter that did not appear pristinely Indian was vastly more complex and required the employment of a variety of techniques.

Curtis's control of his imagery began with his choice of subject matter and presentation. This choice is only implied in the photographs he selected to present to the public—we see what he chose to include in the frame but not what he decided to exclude. The choice of exclusion becomes more explicit, however, when we examine some of the other techniques he used.

Cropping, another means of controlling subject matter, takes place in the darkroom after the negative has been made. If Curtis found something along the edges of the frame which detracted from the image he was trying to create, he could choose to crop it off and print only the remainder of the negative. Unlike framing, in the initial exposure, cropping, in the making of a print, left evidence in the negative of what Curtis had decided to exclude. Occasionally Curtis had several different croppings printed from the same negative. For example, he photographed Chief Joseph and another Nez Perce man sitting in chairs, with Curtis's friend Edmund Meany (a professor of history at the University of Washington) standing behind them. [37] In the version reproduced in *The North American Indian* Meany and the Nez Perce man have been cropped away, leaving only a portrait of Chief Joseph. [38] *Typical Apache* presents yet another example of cropping. As a newspaper account contemporary with the making of this image describes, "From the country of the Apache Mr. Curtis claims to have brought home portraits of some of the most bloodstained individuals of a notoriously bloodstained tribe."[69] The full negative of *Typical Apache* shows the subject standing at an angle to the camera, his right hand placed behind his hip as if reaching for a weapon. The edge of the muslin backdrop of Curtis's studio tent is clearly visible running down the left side of the frame, thus indicating that this image was formally posed and therefore diminishing its impact. [39] As this image appears in *The North American Indian*, it has been cropped inward from both sides: the edge

[37] Chief Joseph, Edmund Meany, and
Unidentified Nez Perce Indian
Edward Curtis

Chief Joseph has become famous among
Whites because of his attempt to lead the
Nez Perce to Canada in order to escape
confinement on a reservation. The attempt
failed when the Nez Perce were ambushed by
the U.S. Army near the Canadian border.
Professor Edmund Meany taught history at
the University of Washington and was a
close friend of Curtis's.

of the muslin backdrop is removed and the subject forced visually forward at the viewer. [40]

Curtis's use of posing was central to the creation of his imagery of Indianness. The entry for "money paid to Indians," which appeared in Curtis's proposal for funding from J. P. Morgan, reappears in each of his successive funding requests. Payment of his subjects for posing was a routine practice. George Wharton James, one of the most thoughtful and enlightened ethnographic photographers at the turn of the century, wrote a piece for *Camera Craft* on "The Study of Indian Faces," in which he commented on the effects of posing:

A "posed" Indian is seldom a natural Indian. The American world has greatly admired the fine photographs of Indians made by a famous photographer and yet they are no more true to life than are the bridal photographs true to the everyday life of the woman who has just settled down to the duties of her household life, and soon becomes the active bustling mother of a family. Both photographs—fancy Indian and bridal— are merely phases. Only during war or on ceremonial occasions is the Indian the befeathered, dressed up, beaded, fringed, fantastic individual the celebrated photographer represents him to be. And, as these photographs were made away from the natural surroundings of the Indians, they are not true to life.[70]

Although James does not mention the "famous photographer" by name, the criticism directly applies to Curtis's approach to his work. When Curtis paid a subject to pose for his camera, the subject temporarily became his employee, and doubtless felt obliged to pose either in a fashion directed by Curtis or at least in one appealing to his sense of imagery. Subjects presented themselves to the camera more as what Curtis imagined they *should* be than as what they *felt* or actually *were*. In terms of pictorialist aesthetics, posing contributed positively to the final image. In terms of ethnography, posing did "injustice to scientific accuracy."

One of the more striking examples of posing subjects occurred while Curtis was making photographs of Navajos, which he eventually used in volume one of *The North American Indian*. Returning to Seattle from the Southwest, Curtis boasted to a reporter for the *Seattle Times* that he had managed to photograph the sacred Navajo Yebechai Dance, despite advice from ethnographers at the Smithsonian Institution that it could not be done. The account of Curtis's efforts published by the *Times* is enlightening, not only in

[38] CHIEF JOSEPH—NEZ PERCE
Edward Curtis

Curtis created this portrait of Chief Joseph—used as an illustration in *The North American Indian*—by merely changing his framing to exclude Edmund Meany and the other unidentified Nez Perce man.

terms of the use of posing, but also of his willingness to make and use props:

After Curtis had gone more miles than he has hairs on his head—and he isn't very bald except in front—he came to a little store kept by a white man, "Charlie," and who has lived and traded among the Navajos for the last forty years. When he stated his mission, Charlie told him frankly that to get that dance he would have to break down a barrier of

[39]

[40]

superstition and fanatical belief that it had taken decades upon decades to build. However, Charlie promised all the aid in his power, and it was largely to his efforts that the Curtis expedition proved a success.

The story of how Curtis finally won over the fourteen men, requirements of the dance calling for that number, will probably never be told. To those fourteen Indians the dance was the most solemn event in their lives. In the first place according to the dictations of the gods of wind, water, and air, the dance should never be held until after the first frost of the fall. Again, it was heap big bad medicine for a white man to watch the wild gyrations of the dancers, and again the figures must be danced when the blackness of the night is upon the face of the earth. Last, but not least, the masks must never, under any circumstances, fall into the hands of strangers.

Curtis as a God

And when a man, no matter of what nationality, goes directly against his god, the power that compels him must be strong indeed. In this instance, Curtis declares his power was not money. Perhaps Curtis with his rumpled hair and blonde Vandyke beard was to those fourteen Indians the moon god, or a star god, but whoever they took him to be he got results, and that was what he sought.

To begin with, Curtis got the favor of three Indians, the same three that later posed for him before their sacred shrine. He then rented a closed room over Charlie's store. For days and days Curtis was busy making the fourteen masks necessary for the dance. Do you suppose for an instant that those three Indians would have anything to do with the making of those masks? Not much. As Harry Hayward thought it no sin to plan a murder so long as he did not personally commit the crime, so did those Indians dodge the religious sin they were committing, by telling

[39] TYPICAL APACHE (full-frame)

[40] TYPICAL APACHE (cropped)

Edward Curtis

In the full-frame version of this image, Curtis's use of his studio tent and muslin backdrop are clearly obvious. With the image cropped, as it appeared in *The North American Indian,* the studio environment is less noticeable. The cropping makes this image seem menacing and creates an allusion to stereotypes of the Apache as bloodthirsty. It visually compresses the subject, forcing him forward at the viewer so that his quarter profile stance appears as a crouch.

Curtis how to do the work, although they never lifted a finger to assist him, nor did they touch the masks until the day they were donned and the dance began.

During the mask making season, Curtis gradually spread the power of his mystic charm until he had secured enough Indians to carry out his plans. There was not an Indian who gave the secret away, nor one who did not consent to the scheme, although in some instances, it took days and days in convincing the doubting one that Curtis was that mysterious someone who should be obeyed. Of course, money might have helped some, but money was not in the running with those long bolts of bright red and blue calico that Curtis had securely tucked away in his saddle bags. [41–42]

Curiosity Aroused

The fact that Curtis remained closeted with three Indians in a small hot room over the store, aroused a great deal of curiosity among the Indians who were not on the inside. They were continually hanging around just outside the door, and whenever Curtis or one of his three assistants would leave the room, a dozen pairs of prying eyes stole glances through the hastily shut door.

Of course, the Indians at first never dreamed that their brother redskins were giving away the secrets of the Yabachi [*sic*] dance. That was probably the last thing that occurred to them. But gradually, as the days wore on, there came a suspicion that aroused the Indians to the heights of frenzy.

"What did they do?" asked his interviewer, when Mr. Curtis reached this point in his story.

"Well, as near as I recollect it, they raised merry hell."

Held A Powwow

Up to that time, the Indians had dead sure evidence against only two of the fourteen who eventually tripped with bare feet through the sacred dance. And for the greater part of a night those two certainly were the pivotal center of a busy scene.

The big powwow was held on the front veranda of Charlie's store, and Curtis was a mighty interested onlooker. First one chief would get up and spill Navajo adjectives over a big part of the reservation, and he would be followed by another and another until a new day had dawned over the foothills of the east.

But the two Indians "stood pat." And when it was seen that protests, threats and pleadings came to nothing, two of the Indians secured the fleetest ponies of the ranch and put off at high speed to tell their tale to the Indian agent.

It was then that Curtis knew he had won. It was a good day's ride to

[41]

[42]

[41] HASCHEBAAD—NAVAHO

[42] HASCHELTI—NAVAHO

Edward Curtis

These two portraits depict dancers in the Yebechai ceremony. According to a newspaper article based on an interview with Curtis, the Yebechai dancers were extremely nervous about being photographed. They therefore insisted that Curtis make their costumes himself so that the clothing would not have a religious significance.

the Indian agent, and that meant the passing of two days before the messengers could return. As everything was in readiness for the dance Curtis did not delay another moment. As soon as the crowd had drifted away, Curtis put off for the mountains. When he started he could not see one of the "faithful fourteen," and as a matter of fact, he did not know whether he would ever see them again or not.

Charlie was with him, and by and by they came to a little wooded, grass covered ravine in the heart of the foothills. "Put your camera up there," said Charlie, and when that had been done they seated themselves and waited.

The Dancers Appear

It wasn't very long before Curtis saw that he was not to be disappointed. Down the ravine came fourteen of the queerest, most fantastically dressed figures Curtis ever saw in his life. It would be impossible to describe the dance. The camera alone has the power to do that, but Edward S. Curtis of Seattle saw what no other white man had seen before.[71] [43]

Even the most sensitive ethnographers of the period were capable of resorting to trickery in attempts to learn the secrets of Indian traditions, but few were as casual about it as Curtis. Behavior such as that attributed to Curtis in photographing the Yebechai dance not only engendered mistrust among the people he worked with but was also irresponsible ethnography. Given his manipulation of his subjects, the resulting photographs were often inaccurate.

In addition to the inaccuracies which Curtis himself created, his subjects sometimes felt obliged to introduce inaccuracies of their own. Dr. William B. Lee, anthropologist and director of the Los Angeles County Museum of Natural History, tells of having brought a copy of volume one of *The North American Indian* (which includes photographs of the Yebechai Dance) and a print of *Shadowcatchers* (a recent film by T. C. McCluhan which includes footage of the Yebechai Dance shot by Curtis) to show to Navajos at their tribal museum. Among the Navajos present were a number of men who were themselves Yebechai dancers. After seeing the depiction of the dance in *Shadowcatchers,* these men approached Dr. Lee and reported that Curtis had not recorded the dance exactly as it was supposed to be. The dance, which has a specific directional orientation, was being performed backwards in the film. Dr. Lee suggested that McCluhan had simply flopped the print (printed it backwards). The dancers indicated that they

[43] YEBECHAI PRAYER—NAVAHO
Edward Curtis

Curtis posed this enactment of the Yebechai ceremony. Probably without Curtis's knowledge, the dancers performed the dance backwards in order to secularize it.

doubted this explanation because the dancers in the film appeared not to know the dance very well, as they were unusually clumsy and kept bumping into each other. A comparison of the film with the still photographs in *The North American Indian* confirmed that the stills too were reversed. The modern Navajo dancers then suggested to Dr. Lee that the dancers whom Curtis had employed had not wanted a sacred dance to be filmed, and had therefore secularized it by dancing it backwards.[72]

X3442-12

[44] QUILEUTE GIRL
Edward Curtis

Curtis's fabrication of costumes for his subjects was not always so
complex as the making of Yebechai masks. The subject in this image
prominently displays a shawl with a machine-stitched seam, indicating
that the item may in fact have been a canvas tarp.

Posing and the use of props were techniques common in pictorial photography, and Curtis's skill with them was an important
factor in bringing public attention to his work. [44] Retouching
was another technique often used in pictorial photography (although purists—"straight" photographers—such as Alfred Stieglitz objected to its use as "unphotographic"). Retouching had
been practiced since the early days of photography, but had come
into vogue during the 1860s when the standard format for commercial portrait photography had grown from the carte de visite to
the cabinet photograph.[73] Although not nearly as subtle as the
airbrush retouching now in use, retouching had already been
refined considerably by the turn of the century and could be
practiced in a variety of ways. In its simplest form retouching was
done on the negative itself by using a stylus or abrasive on the
emulsion to add details, or a retouching pencil to change or
remove them. Retouching was also done by painting or drawing
on a print and then rephotographing the print to create a negative
which incorporated the retouching. When, as was the case with
the reproduction of photographs in *The North American Indian,*
images were printed in photogravure, another opportunity for
retouching was introduced.

Photogravures were prints in ink made from a steel-faced copper plate. Through use of a photochemical acid engraving process,
these plates were made from a glass-plate positive of a photograph. The effect of this engraving process was to create pinprick
concavities in the plate surface which retained ink, much like
hand engraving. By engraving or abrading by hand, dark areas
could be created.

Under his direction, Curtis's lab assistants and gravure printers
extensively used all of these techniques. Highlights were added
and tonal qualities altered in many, if not most, of Curtis's portraits. Writing in *Camera Craft* in 1906, Curtis's lab assistant
Adolf F. Muhr described this practice:

Have you ever watched the affectionate care with which an artist puts
the finishing touches on his painting? Adding a high light here and a dark
touch there by way of accentuation is all he does. That is all that is
required in our work, a touch here and there.[74]

A touch here and there may have been all that was required in
Muhr's work for Curtis, but it was by no means all that he did.
[45–54] Presumably under Curtis's direction, Muhr retouched a

[45] ON THE LITTLE BIGHORN
Edward Curtis

In this romantically composed pictorial a wagon has been removed by retouching. The scratchy marks of the retouching stylus are visible just to the left of the center of the frame.

[46] FIESTA OF SAN ESTEVAN
Edward Curtis

In this image made at Acoma Pueblo hats and suspenders were retouched away.

[47] FIESTA OF SAN ESTEVAN
Edward Curtis

In another view of the festival, close inspection reveals that through retouching two parasols have been removed from just above center frame.

[48] ASSINIBOIN CAMP ON BOW RIVER
Edward Curtis

The lodges depicted in this image were made from machine-woven fabric, possibly feed sacks. Close inspection shows retouching marks where product labels were removed.

[49] PIMA WATER GIRL
Edward Curtis

The woman depicted here was dipping water from an irrigation ditch when photographed. Crosshatching on the negative with a retouching stylus makes the ditch appear to be a pond.

[50] NAVAHO FLOCKS
Edward Curtis

Given the lengths to which Curtis went to remove subject matter suggesting the influence of White culture, it seems strange that he showed a flock of sheep. Although sheep had been introduced to the Navajo by Whites, most Whites thought of them as typical aspects of Navajo life. Apparently sheep didn't strike Curtis as "un-Indian."

[51] BEAD FLOWER ("KWAA-POUI")—TEWA
Edward Curtis

Jewelry was also popularly thought to be typically "Indian." The
brooches worn by the subject of this image, however, appear to have
been made by Whites. Interestingly, the brooches contained photographic
miniature portraits.

[52] DRINK IN THE DESERT
Edward Curtis

This image was as much drawn as it was photographed. Ironically,
although horses—like sheep—were introduced to Indians by Whites,
these animals too had been incorporated into stereotypes of
"Indianness."

[53] NIGHT SCOUT—NEZ PERCE
Edward Curtis

This photograph was actually made in broad daylight. The illusion of a
dark sky was created either by scraping the emulsion away from the
area of the sky in the negative or by painting on a print and
rephotographing the print.

[54] FIRING POTTERY
Edward Curtis

This image was originally entitled *Preparing Wedding Feast*. The pot, which
makes the present title seem justified, was added with a retouching stylus.

variety of objects out of his images. Generally the objects removed were of White manufacture. Among these were wagons, parasols, hats, suspenders, and product labels. Apparently such retouching was done in an effort to be "truthful" according to the ethnocentric conception of the ethnographic present. Being of White manufacture, the objects removed were evidence of the acculturation of the subjects and would have detracted from the conformity of the photographs to imagery of "Indianness."

Assuming that adherence to the ethnographic present, and not simple deception, was Curtis's motivation for retouching, it is interesting to note other evidence of acculturation left untouched. Machine-woven fabrics, rifles, medals and other jewelry of White manufacture, sheep, and horses all appear frequently. These items, unlike those which Curtis had retouched out of his photographs, were all common in popular imagery of "Indianness" and therefore would not have appeared out of place to most Whites. Curtis was aware that these objects had been introduced by Whites, but he included them anyway. Given his hope for *The North American Indian* that "neither the pictures nor the descriptive matter will be found lacking in popular interest," and his frequent lack of reverence for scientific detail, it seems that indeed truthfulness to imagery was more important to Curtis than truthfulness to the people and cultures he photographed.

Removal of unwanted detail was certainly not the only end toward which Curtis employed retouching. When it came to pictorialist aesthetics, he was dedicated in his pursuit of dramatic effect. If an image seemed bland for lack of clouds in the sky, then clouds were created; if an image lacked sufficient contrast, retouching could correct this too.

In other technical choices Curtis also opted for the creation of dramatic effect over representation in maximum detail. Many of his images are not in sharp focus. Curtis's mastery of camera technique was profound, and he was certainly capable of focusing a camera. Not the result of carelessness, the use of soft focus was a conscious choice to create a romantic feel in a photograph similar to that in an impressionist painting. In a similar vein Curtis frequently used a large lens aperture. The size of lens aperture governs the depth of field. The larger the lens opening, the shallower the depth of field. By using a very large opening Curtis ensured that only that on which he focused would appear in sharp detail, while the rest of the image would be blurred. Sometimes

when using a large lens opening, he focused on an object in the foreground or background, leaving the subject of the photograph in fuzzy soft focus. In such cases, like *The Storm—Apache,* the choice of pictorial effect rather than concern for ethnographic documentation is explicit. [55] Curtis also used depth of field to exclude unintended subject matter. If he could not exclude the unwanted subject matter in the background through framing, he could use a large lens opening to render the background in indistinct blur.

In his general introduction to *The North American Indian* Curtis wrote that "while primarily a photographer, I do not see or think photographically; hence the story of Indian life will not be told in microscopic detail, but rather will be presented as a broad and luminous picture." He seems to be alluding to the still popular stereotype of the time, which held that photography was a mechanistic medium mired in excessive detail. Given Curtis's use of soft focus, it might have been more accurate for him to have said: I do not see or think like an ethnographic documentarist . . . but rather like a romantic pictorialist photographer.

Curtis *was* primarily a photographer, but following his work on the text of the first two volumes of *The North American Indian,* it appears that he became almost exclusively a photographer—although he was also an administrator and publicist. Of the drafts and notes for *The North American Indian* submitted to Fredrick Webb Hodge for editing, those for the first two volumes appear largely in Curtis's rather impressionistic style. Most of the remainder, except for those relating to the last two volumes, are in a tighter, more scientific style. In a letter to Hodge in 1907, Curtis implied how this drift away from work on the text may have begun. Frustrated by a delay caused when his son, who was visiting him "in the field," contracted typhoid, Curtis wrote that "I am trying to figure a way to offset this delay and thought I might do it by skimming the work on a couple of reservations and get[ting] someone to take up the detail work for me."[75] Apparently Curtis went considerably beyond acquiring "someone to take up the detail work." According to Hodge, it was in fact Curtis's most faithful field assistant, William E. Myers, who wrote most of the text for *The North American Indian.*[76] Judging on the basis of style and content, it would seem that Curtis continued to write introductions to each volume and captions for the images in the accompanying portfolios. But even when the text was written by

[55] THE STORM—APACHE
Edward Curtis

This image demonstrates a technique used frequently by Curtis to the detriment of his photographs' usefulness as documents. The use of a large aperture, or lens opening, limits the depth of field so that only a small part of the subject is in focus, leaving the rest blurred. Curtis sometimes used this technique to obscure objects that he could not avoid including in the frame.

others, Curtis remained the authority under whose supervision the work was carried out. With the text, as with lab work on his photographs, Curtis was willing to delegate authority. But it was under his name that the products were published, and the work of his assistants was consistent with the philosophical tone set in the first two volumes.

The reception which greeted volume one upon publication was mixed. While Curtis continued to enjoy the favor of his lay audience, he began to encounter doubts among those to whom he referred as the "serious minded." These doubts generally focused on the magnitude of the project.[77] Ethnographers versed in the difficulties of original field work were skeptical that Curtis could cover an area of such breadth without merely restating the research of others.

Curtis was concerned about criticism of *The North American Indian* by professional ethnologists. He explained away their skepticism, however, as a reaction to inflated accounts of his work in the popular press. He complained in a letter to Hodge that "you can understand readily that when a newspaper starts to do a thing, they are much inclined to over-do it." If this was the case, it was to some extent the result of Curtis's own promotion, as he and his publicists often fostered the writing of such extravagant accounts themselves.[78] He appears to have understood his dilemma and wrote again to Hodge:

Unfortunately for our feelings, at times, this book must be sold. The majority of the buyers of it are the ones who may be influenced by more or less of a glowing account of the work, while this same thing would cause a feeling of resentment on the part of others, and those then being the ones that we want the good will of more than anyone else.

. . . It will not be necessary, of course, to explain to them that the work is not intended wholly for the scientific reader, but rather to make a lasting picture of the Indian, showing as much of the beautiful of his way of life as we can. . . .[79]

Stated more baldly, Curtis was selling images to a popular audience whose perception of "Indianness" was based on stereotypes. Further, that audience was also aware—with whatever lack of subtlety—of ethnographic science, and in order for Curtis's salesmanship to be effective, it was very important that he remain in the good graces of professional ethnographers. Whereas ethnographers themselves were often susceptible to ethnocentric stereotypes, they were becoming more careful in the exercise of their discipline, and few professionals indulged in the extremities of artistic license characteristic of Curtis's work.

Having gotten himself into this dilemma through his efforts at public relations, Curtis attempted to mollify his critics by the same means, telling Hodge that

you will have a chance from time to time to drop a good word in regard to the book, and, as you say, it is of course, to your interest that we get it on the best possible footing. And while I do not believe that we need apologize to anyone for the first two volumes, I do feel that every volume we bring together will be better than the one before. . . .[80]

Only a few professional ethnographers were openly hostile toward Curtis and his work, and there were at least as many who continued to offer praise. Production of *The North American Indian* moved ahead at a brisk pace, and by 1909 the first four volumes had been published.

Volume one was devoted to the Apache and the Navajo, and the text often reflects the informal style representative of Curtis's early research. Relating his experiences while accompanying a group of Apaches on their yearly mescal harvest, Curtis described a young girl preparing for bed—"Little Miss Apache, sitting in the middle of the blanket with her knees drawn up to her chin and with scant skirt now tucked carefully about her feet looks up with roguish smile, then down at her wriggling toes in defiance."[81] The drafts for this volume contain numerous references to Curtis's attempts to buy information, most of which were edited before publication. The published text does, however, describe his purchase of a maternity belt from an Apache woman:

The owner of this particular belt, a widow, did not care to dispose of it; as she expressed it, "it is like a husband to me"; the remuneration from the granting of its use was sufficient to support her.[82]

Curtis was not always completely unscientific, nor was he entirely unappreciative of the accomplishments of the people he described.

Civilized women may write books, paint pictures, or deliver ringing addresses, these are unknown worlds to the Navaho women; but when after months of labor she finishes a blanket, her pride in her work of art is well justified.[83]

Even at its most scientific and sympathetic, however, the text of volume one was still prone to stereotype and reflected the tendency of the period toward simplistic Darwinian analysis:

The clan and gentile systems of the American Indians have been the bulwark of their social structure, for by preventing inter-marriage within the clan of gens the blood was kept at its best. Added to this were the hardships of Indian life, which resulted in survival of only the fittest and provided the foundation for a sturdy people. But with advancing civilization one foresees the inevitable disintegration of their tribal laws, and a consequent weakening of the entire social structure, for the Indians seem to have absorbed all the evil and to have embodied little of the good that civilized life teaches.[84]

The photogravures illustrating volume one concentrate on pictorial splendor, and offer little documentation of the lives of their subjects. In conjunction, however, with the portfolio of images which accompanies the volume, the photogravures do serve to introduce many of the pictorial genres that occur in the rest of *The North American Indian.*

Portfolio one opens with *The Vanishing Race—Navaho,* a nostalgic pictorial which alludes to Curtis's belief in Manifest Destiny. [56] In his caption to this image he described its intent:

The thought which this picture is meant to convey is that the Indians as a race, already shorn of their tribal strength and stripped of their primitive dress, are passing into the darkness of an unknown future. Feeling that the picture expresses so much of the thought that inspired the entire work, the author has chosen it as the first of the series.

In an article published in *Scribner's Magazine* the previous year, Curtis had offered a broader description of his ideas about Manifest Destiny.

It is true that advancement demands the extermination of these wild, care-free, picturesque Indians, and, in the language of our President [Roosevelt], we cannot keep them or their lands for bric-a-brac. The fact that we cannot, however, makes it nonetheless regrettable or hard on the people who are being ground beneath the wheel of civilization, and though we may be able to justify our claims that advancement and progress demand the extermination of the Indians, we can scarcely justify the method used in this extermination.

Curtis continued, blaming "unscrupulous politicians" for White behavior toward Indians, but at the same time he voiced his belief in Indian inferiority by patronizingly comparing them with children.

As the years pass on and we are able to see this subject as history, stripped of its little local prejudices, we will be found guilty as a nation, under the manipulations of crafty, unscrupulous politicians, of having committed more than "the crime of a century." In all our years of handling the Indians we have taught them one thing—the white man seldom told the truth. The relationship of the Indians and people of this country is that of a child and parent. We will stand convicted for all time as a parent who failed in his duty.[85]

[56] THE VANISHING RACE—NAVAHO
Edward Curtis

Curtis wrote in the caption for this image, "Feeling that the picture
expresses so much of the thought that inspired the entire work, the
author has chosen it as the first of the series." There is in this romantic
pictorial an allusion to Manifest Destiny. A line of Indians crosses a
murky foreground (metaphorically, the present) toward a threatening wall
of darkness (the future). Above the darkness is an aura of light (Curtis's
hope for "improvement" of Indians through assimilation into White
culture). *The Vanishing Race—Navaho* also foreshadows Curtis's "entire
work" in another way: it is heavily retouched.

The Vanishing Race—Navaho succeeds in expressing these
thoughts visually. A line of Indians diagonally traverses a murky
foreground (the present) toward a threatening wall of darkness
(the future) above which is an aura of light (Curtis's hope for
improvement of Indians through assimilation into White culture).
Curtis's artistic treatment of this gravure also foreshadows his
"entire work" by stressing pictorial effect above ethnographic
documentation. *The Vanishing Race—Navaho* is as much the
result of retouching as it is a product of the original negative. The
sticks in the lower right-hand corner were apparently enhanced by
strokes of a stylus, and the shapes of the Indian riders were
defined by highlights which were enhanced with a negative retouching pencil. Even the hopeful aura of light running along the
horizon was retouched into the image.

The gravure which follows *The Vanishing Race—Navaho* also
indicates Curtis's conception of his work in its appeal to popular
imagery of "Indianness." Plate two is a portrait of Geronimo, the
Apache whose reputation as a murderous "renegade" was based
more on White legends than on fact. [57] In his caption, Curtis
describes how the original negative for this heavily retouched
gravure was made:

The picture was taken at Carlisle, Pennsylvania [site of a U.S. government Indian school], the day before the inauguration of President Roosevelt, Geronimo being one of the warriors who took part in the inaugural
parade at Washington. He appreciated the honor of being one of those
chosen for this occasion, and the catching of his features while the old
warrior was in a retrospective mood was most fortunate.

The Apache stands as yet another example of Curtis's fondness
for pictorial generalization. Much as he was able to perceive tribal
variation among Indians and still remain preoccupied with what
he believed to be racial characteristics, Curtis frequently sub-
merged his recognition of individual variation in a tendency toward tribal stereotypes. Typing according to race or tribe was not
unique to Curtis; in his willingness to engage in visual stereotypes
of tribal characteristics, he probably believed himself to be building on strong scientific foundations.

During the late nineteenth century, researchers whose legitimacy as "scientists" was widely accepted had become obsessed
with the attempt to correlate physical characteristics with tendencies in bahavior. Physiognomists sometimes attempted to link
behavior to facial characteristics, and craniologists often tried to

prove the legitimacy of their belief in racial hierarchies of intelligence through measurement of the cranial capacity of skulls. The larger the average skull size, they supposed, the more intelligent the "race." Despite massive inconsistencies in the results and the absurdity of many of the premises, the conclusions of such racially bigoted "science" had a widespread impact on both popular and scientific thinking.[86]

In the measurement of human bodies, or anthropometry, as it was called, photography was often employed as a means of making visual records. Anthropometric photography, though often independent of the extremes of "scientific" racism, could also frequently provide the vehicle for racial and cultural stereotypes. By the turn of the century, anthropometric photography had been reduced to a generally standardized format. This format included at least two portraits, one full frontal, and one in profile, usually shot against a neutral background.

The Apache, like many of Curtis's early tribal stereotypes, did not conform to anthropometric conventions in that its subject is depicted against a romantically pictorial setting. [58] Later in his work Curtis used the standard formula of front and side portraits more frequently. He continued, however, to make pictorials that were intended to convey broad generalizations about tribal appearance and character. Curtis wrote of *The Apache* that "this picture might be titled 'Life Primeval,'" indicating that its purpose was to convey a feeling for what he imagined as primitiveness. Photographed with his back to the camera, the subject is naked except for a breechclout and a head cloth. He stands, as Curtis wrote, "at a spot on Black River, Arizona, where the dark, still pool breaks into the laugh of a rapids." In the context of Curtis's oft-stated opinions about the effects on Indians of contact with White culture, the "dark, still pool" could be interpreted as a metaphor for the stagnation of "savagery," whereas the "laugh of a rapids" might be thought to represent "improvement" through "civilization."

Volume two, which appeared in 1908, is a broad catch-basket of other southwestern Indian cultures, including the Pima, Papago, Kwatika, Mohave, Yuma, Maricopa, Walapai, Havasupai, and Apache-Mohave (Yavapai). The text for this volume devotes a great deal of attention to the histories of these tribes since contact with Whites. Interestingly, this is quite characteristic of the text—though Curtis desired that it not be so of the photographs—for the entire series. Possible explanations for this dichotomy between

[57] GERONIMO—APACHE
Edward Curtis

Geronimo's reputation as a murderous "renegade" was based more on White legends than on fact. Curtis photographed him at the U.S. Indian school in Carlisle, Pennsylvania, just before Geronimo participated in Theodore Roosevelt's inauguration as president. This image is also heavily retouched.

[58] THE APACHE
Edward Curtis

In addition to reinforcing stereotypes about Indians as a "race," Curtis also made stereotypes of tribes. This romantic pictorial is an example of just such a tribal stereotype. Later in his work Curtis's tribal "types" alluded more often to scientific (anthropometric) photography by his use of a standard combination of front and profile portraits.

text and illustration are numerous, although Curtis never offered a definitive explanation of his own. It seems likely that the audience for whom the pictorial imagery was appealing was only marginally interested in the text. If they read the text at all, they were less likely to be offended by a verbal breach of their ideas of "Indianness" than they would have been by a pictorial breach. The public still believed in the fiction that photographs never lied. Ironically, popular illusions about "Indianness" were so ingrained that had Curtis's images been more accurate, his audience would most likely have thought them to be lying.

In volume two there is even some pictorial recognition of acculturation in the photographs of the mission of San Xavier Del Bac, perhaps because the antiquity of the mission made it seem an admissible subject. [59] According to Curtis:

These various tribes have been broadly termed, with the Pueblos, the sedentary Indians of the Southwest. Most of them came early in direct contact with Spanish missionaries, whose ministrations they received in friendly spirit; yet after more than two centuries of zealous effort, little has been accomplished toward substituting the religion of the white man for that of their fathers. True, many are professed adherents of the Christian faith, but only in rare instances has an Indian really abandoned his own gods. As a rule the extent of their Christianization has been their willingness to add another god to their pantheon.[87]

Curtis's descriptions of the tribes in this volume were riddled with some of the most extreme examples of his tendency toward tribal stereotype. He repeatedly used the words "superior" or "inferior," implying but never explicitly stating his belief that tribes, like "races," could be hierarchically ranked. Of the Mohave, he wrote:

Physically the Mohave are probably superior to any other tribe in the United States. Man and women alike are big-boned, well knitted, clear skinned. Mentally they are dull and slow—brothers to the ox.

To explain their supposed stupidity, Curtis relied on the idea—more prevalent in the eighteenth and nineteenth centuries—that local environment determined inheritance.

The warm climate and comparative ease with which they obtain their livelihood seem to have developed a people physically superb; but the climate and conditions that developed such magnificent bodies did not demand or assist in the building up of an equivalent mentality.[88]

[59] MISSION SAN XAVIER DEL BAC
Edward Curtis

Curtis presumably included this image in *The North American Indian* because of the long history of contact between Pueblo Indians and the Catholic Church. The mission also had great appeal as pictorial subject matter.

84

X2141-07

[60] THE MOHAVE
Edward Curtis

Describing in *The North American Indian*
the tribe of which this image is a
stereotype, Curtis offered an example of his
prejudice toward his subjects. "Physically
the Mohave are probably superior to any
other tribe in the United States. Men and
women alike are big-boned, well knitted,
clear skinned. Mentally they are dull and
slow—brothers to the ox." In his frequent
use of the words "superior" and "inferior"
to describe tribes, Curtis implied that he
believed that tribes, like "races," could be
ranked hierarchically.

The Mohave is the pictorial embodiment of Curtis's stereotype of this tribe. [60] Standing at a quarter angle to the camera, the subject presents his "physically superior" back as he gazes over the bank of the Colorado River. The subject was posed to affect "Indianness" as is indicated by the fact that he is nearly naked. Curtis himself admitted that "at present the men wear fanciful combinations of white men's clothing, usually a pair of overalls and a tight-fitting shirt, which is always painted, sometimes black, sometimes in stripes of several colors."[89] He framed this image so that the horizon line bisects the subject at his shoulders, thus emphasizing his strength but visually severing his head from his body. On the page facing *The Mohave*, Curtis elaborates:

The hour is the end of day; its spell is over the earth. The sun in a sea of gold and crimson is sinking behind mountain crests of copper hue; the shadows are creeping stealthily across sierra, valley, and plain; motionless our giant bronze Mohave is watching the scene as his forefathers for generation after generation watched the same sunsets and the same river flow. Does the gorgeous coloring of yonder clouds, the current of the stream, and the spell of the hour mean anything to him? Perhaps far more than we dream. Ask him, he could not tell; but take him from it and he would die of longing.[90]

In *A Yuma Type* Curtis alludes more directly to standard anthropometric style. [61] Photographed against the neutral backdrop of the Curtis studio tent, the subject confronts the camera with a frontal pose. It is not clear whether the subject affected a plaintive expression in return for payment from Curtis. But Curtis did, however, choose the moment of exposure—what photographer Henri Cartier-Bresson has since referred to as "the decisive moment"—and because of that choice the Yuma are stereotyped in this image as wistful. Given the control over lighting, which his studio tent afforded, Curtis also chose the dramatically raked light in which this portrait was made. Side lighting such as this obscured one side of the subject's face, leaving his features less perceptible and reducing the anthropometric motivation to one merely of nostalgic appearance.

The wistfulness of *A Yuma Type* seems to refer to the regret stimulated in Curtis by his belief that his subject's race was vanishing. It certainly does not correspond with his sensational descriptions of the Yumas' "primitive" militarism:

Warfare against neighboring tribes was carried on more for the purpose of establishing prestige and cultivating prowess than for direct gain, yet

[61] A YUMA TYPE
Edward Curtis

In this tribal "type," Curtis alluded to frontal anthropometric photography. Curtis commonly paid his subjects to pose, and this man's wistful expression may have been affected at Curtis's request. Strong side lighting leaves half of the subject's face in shadow, contributing to the aesthetic appeal of the image, but detracting from its scientific usefulness.

the Yuma never let pass an opportunity to capture children and hold them for ransom. The standard price was two ponies and a blanket.[91]

This account of the holding of children for ransom was probably accurate; but it is also typical of Curtis's preoccupation with any behavior that conformed to prevailing stereotypes of Indians as "hostile savages." He often indulged that preoccupation—both in his photographs and in his writing—with highly speculative observations.

The Northwest Plains Indian is, to the average person, the typical American Indian, the Indian of our schoolday books—powerful of physique, statuesque, gorgeous in dress, with the bravery of the firm believer in predestination. The constant slaughtering of the buffalo trained him to the greatest physical endurance, and gave an inbred desire for bloodshed.[92]

This passage not only reiterates Curtis's belief in the inheritance of acquired characteristics, it also implies that he was sufficiently aware of stereotypes of "Indianness" to be conscious of the fact that he was pandering to them.

Volume three of *The North American Indian* concentrates on tribes of the Rocky Mountains and the Great Plains commonly known as the Teton Sioux, including, as explained by Curtis, "the Ogalala, Brule, Miniconjou, Two Kettle, Sans Arc, Hunkpapa, Blackfoot or Sihasapa, and Yanktonai tribes or bands of the Dakota, and their ethnically close relatives, the Assiniboin."[93] These were the Indians "of our schoolday books," to whose "inbred desire for bloodshed" Curtis had referred, and volume three shows evidence of the pervasive White obsession with their military activities—real and imagined. The volume opens with an introduction by Curtis, which is again largely devoted to expression of his stereotypes. "In gathering the lore of the Indian of the plains," he wrote,

one hears only of yesterday. His thoughts are of the past; today is but a living death, and his very being is permeated with the hopelessness of tomorrow . . . . The younger man, if a true Indian, is a living regret that he is not of the time when to be an Indian was to be a man.[94]

While there was certainly some truth to this observation, he then went on to bemoan the fate of the Plains Indians. Again he blamed that fate on "Nature's laws." In this case, however, Curtis attempted to qualify his attribution of blame. "That the inevitable transformation of the Indian life has been made many-fold harder by the white man's cupidity," he wrote, "there is no

question." Still appealing to his readers' sense of guilt, Curtis ended up reverting to the racial bigotries characteristic of his time:

Those who do not comprehend the limitations of primitive people protest, "Why sympathize with the Indians? They now have every opportunity that civilized man has, and more, for the Government grants them lands and renders them aid in many ways." The question might as well be asked, why the man born without eyes does not see. The Indian is an Indian not alone in name and in the pigmentation of his skin or his other physical characteristics. He developed gradually and through the ages to meet the conditions of a harsh environment exceedingly well, but these conditions were so vastly different from those we have thrust upon him that to expect him to become adjusted to the new requirements in a generation or two would be much like expecting of a child the proficiency of ripe manhood . . . .

Of the present condition of the Sioux little that is encouraging can be said. They have small hope for the future, and a people without the courage of hope are indeed a serious problem with which to deal . . . . The younger generation, having no tribal past, may strive to carve a future, and their children, with even less of the instinct of the hunter, will make even better advance; but standing in the way of the present generation and of all generations to come is the fact that they are Indians, and lack by many ages that which is necessary to enable them to meet the competition of the Caucasian race.[95]

For all his expressed racism, Curtis was obviously concerned with the extreme poverty inflicted upon the Dakota tribes. Not surprisingly, however, his pictorial description of these tribes showed nothing of their poverty, concentrating instead on the "true Indian" as imagined from the past. His imagination, like that of most people of the period, seemed preoccupied with images of Dakota "hostility." The caption for *Ogalala War-Party* explains, "Here is depicted a group of Sioux warriors as they appeared in the days of intertribal warfare, carefully making their way down a hillside in the vicinity of the enemy's camp." [62] Ever since the last brutal massacre of Dakota by the U.S. Army at Wounded Knee, South Dakota, in 1890, great emphasis has been given the idea that Dakota militarism predated conflict with Whites. Implied in this emphasis on "intertribal warfare" is the suggestion that the conflict between Whites and the Dakota tribes was the result of inherent Dakota "desire for bloodshed." The text of volume three notes that in the early eighteenth century the Dakota tribes had emigrated from the eastern side of the American continent. "It would be without doubt that the vast herds of buffalo were the cause of their westward movement."[96] It may be that the buffalo herds with their vulnerability to newly mounted hunters were an aspect of what caused this "westward movement." It is more likely, however, that pressures exerted on eastern tribes by White settlement were the most important motivations for emigration during this period. Whatever the causes of the westward compression of Indian populations during the eighteenth and nineteenth centuries, tensions that had not previously existed were introduced in the West. Diverse cultures were brought into contact with each other for the first time. Population densities increased, thus decreasing the availability of natural resources now needed to support a larger number of people. Aware as we now are of the relationship of cultural friction and crowding to aggression, it would hardly seem surprising that the Dakota sometimes fought with the tribes whose lands they were invading. In fact, when warfare broke out between tribes on the Plains—and in all fairness, Curtis did by implication suggest this— it was heavily symbolic and involved less loss of life than did "civilized" warfare. Certainly the Plains tribes were not genetically warlike. Insofar as they engaged in war for the large-scale taking of life, they were protecting themselves from White encroachment and military campaigns.

By the time Curtis photographed the Dakota tribes, close to thirty years had elapsed since warfare had engulfed the Great Plains—with the exception of Wounded Knee, a massacre that can hardly be described as warfare. The caption for *Brule War-Party* explains that "this rhythmic picture shows a party of Brule Sioux reenacting a raid against the enemy." [63] Curtis's rare candor in admitting the posing of this image may represent a concession to one of his most "serious minded" critics, ethnologist James Mooney. During the year prior to publication of volume three, Mooney had objected to the titling of one of the images as *Cheyenne Warrior*, apparently because it inherently suggested that the Cheyenne were still involved in warfare. Mooney, a remarkable figure in American enthnography, was far ahead of his time in his occasional recognition of the absurdity of the theory of the ethnographic present. Defending himself against Mooney's criticism, Curtis in a letter to Fredrick Webb Hodge had again found refuge in stereotype and the ethnographic present. "An Indian of the old days was a warrior 365 days a year . . . . Further, there has [sic] been in the past, and will be in the future many pictures made which will have a general value as

[62] OGALALA WAR-PARTY
Edward Curtis

This posed image introduces Curtis's preoccupation with past military activities of the Great Plains tribes. In this preoccupation Curtis was reflecting popular attitudes in his culture.

Indian pictures, and they will not be used in the book."[97] Curtis was presumably referring to his pictorial appeals to White stereotypes of "Indianness," which ironically comprise a large portion of his illustrations of *The North American Indian* ("the book") and are prominently represented by his posed allusions to Indian "hostility."

Planning a Raid presents a group of Indians on horseback. One Indian holds a rifle. [64] In his caption Curtis blatantly ignored Mooney's criticism and denied that the image was posed. "The

[63] BRULE WAR-PARTY
Edward Curtis

Curtis believed that "the constant slaughtering of the buffalo" had given the Plains tribes "an inbred desire for bloodshed." It is partly because of this belief that he was so fascinated by military activities which the Plains tribes no longer practiced.

[64] PLANNING A RAID
Edward Curtis

Indians, in their striking and characteristic costumes, unconsciously form themselves into most picturesque groups." Curtis stated that the photograph had been taken overlooking Wounded Knee Creek. It seems overwhelmingly insensitive that Curtis, in an image intended to allude to Indian "hostility," positioned the Indians overlooking the point where three hundred Dakota had been massacred by the Hotchkiss guns and carbines of the U.S. Army. His staging of *The Morning Attack* differs from the sham battles of popular Wild West Shows only in its setting, which is against a Plains background rather than an arena in some eastern city. [65]

Volume three, in addition to focusing on "intertribal" warfare, concentrates on White-Indian conflict with a lengthy discussion of the Custer "massacre." By emphasis, this concentration demonstrated a greater concern by Curtis for Indian slaughter of Whites than for the reverse—a slaughter much more prevalent. Although the description of "the Custer fight" was written by his historian friend, Edmund S. Meany, Curtis spent a great deal of time riding over the battlefield in southern Montana trying, with the aid of Custer's Crow Indian scouts, to retrace the action of the battle. At some point during these efforts Curtis was photographed with the scouts in front of a monument erected in Custer's memory. [66]

Volume four, also published in 1909, covered the Crow (or Apsaroke) and the Hidatsa. In linking these two tribes Curtis strayed from his usual groupings according to geography. He explained that this deviation was justified by the extreme ethnic similarity of these tribes. Most of this volume, one of the longest in *The North American Indian*, was devoted to the Crows, of whom Curtis had an unusually high opinion:

In the Apsaroke is seen the highest development of the primitive American hunter and warrior. Physically these people were among the finest specimens of their race. They clothed themselves better and dwelt in larger and finer lodges than did their neighbors, and decked their horses in trappings so gorgeous as to arouse the wonder of all early explorers.[98]

The rifles held by the two subjects on the left are evidence of one of the influences of White culture on the Plains tribes, although not intended as such by Curtis. Plains tribes' warfare prior to contact with Whites was mostly symbolic and involved relatively little loss of life. During westward expansion the Plains tribes were often forced to kill in earnest in order to protect themselves.

[65] THE MORNING ATTACK
Edward Curtis

This staged battle differs from the sham battles of the popular Wild West Shows only in that it took place on the open plains instead of in a stadium or on a playing field.

In addition to their appearance (a boon to Curtis's efforts at popular imagery), the Crows were attractive because of their history of friendliness toward White settlers. Curtis reported that he was "fortunate indeed in enlisting the services of Hunts To Die, a veteran of unusual mentality, from whom was obtained a large part of the information respecting the Apsaroke herein recorded." He also enjoyed assistance from A. B. Upshaw, who was "an interpreter possessing far more than ordinary ability." The help of these assistants, Curtis claimed, allowed "this part of the story of the Indian [to] more closely portray the primitive life than has been possible in the preceding volumes of the series."

Anthropologist Robert Lowie started working with the Crow at about the same time as Curtis was photographing them. In his book *The Crow Indians,* published in 1935, Lowie credited Curtis as an important source of information.

The only previous account known to me of Crow life as a whole is that by Mr. Edward S. Curtis in his "The North American Indian," vol. IV, 1909. It is an excellent piece of work and while not written either by or for a professional anthropologist lives up to high standards of accuracy. The account of the Sun Dance is especially noteworthy. Unfortunately the de luxe make-up of the book has precluded wide circulation.[99]

Considering Curtis's attributions to his assistants (Hunts To Die, Upshaw, and Myers), perhaps they should have received this praise.

Although the text of volume four may indeed have presented a more accurate reconstruction of Crows' lives from the past, the accompanying photographs did not differ significantly in orientation from those of the previous volumes. Curtis's portrait of A. B. Upshaw, made in 1905, depicts him wearing a feather bonnet and ornate necklaces. [67] That this was not his ordinary dress is indicated by another portrait, credited to F. A. Rinehart but probably taken by Curtis's lab assistant, A. F. Muhr. In this portrait, which predates Curtis's by at least seven years, Upshaw appears with his hair neatly combed and wearing a coat and tie. [68]

The feather bonnet in Curtis's version not only looked "Indian" to the casual observer, it also concealed short hair, which did *not* look Indian. Although worn only on rare occasions, feather bonnets appear repeatedly throughout volumes three and four. Because of the use of soft focus and the lack of definition inherent to the gravure printing process, it is usually difficult to make out the fine details of costumery in Curtis's portraits. It appears, however, that the same bonnets and shirts show up repeatedly on individuals of different tribes. [69–70] Since Curtis supplied costumes elsewhere, it is likely that he carried these shirts and bonnets with him to conceal the evidence of acculturation in his subjects.

In the depiction of the Crow, like that of the Dakota, Curtis's imagery focuses heavily on allusion to military activity. Shot from downhill of the subjects, *Apsaroke War Group* and *Ready for the Charge—Apsaroke* use an exaggeratedly low camera angle to lend a monumental appearance to Curtis's tribute to "the highest development of the primitive American hunter and warrior.'' [71–72] Curtis used the same technique in *Crying to the Spirits—Hidatsa*.

The fear of ''pagan'' religions had sometimes been a motivation behind the efforts to exterminate Indians during the eighteenth and nineteenth centuries. Following successful conquest of the continent, however, this fear had softened to the point of viewing Indian religions as mysterious but quaint oddities. While Curtis professed a profound respect for Indian religions, he was not beyond capitalizing on the sense of mysteriousness with which his audience viewed them. *Crying to the Spirits—Hidatsa* also reflects, in addition to a low camera angle, the use of a darkroom technique known as ''burning-in.'' In an unmanipulated print, the sky of this photograph was almost entirely white. [73] In making the print used for reproduction, the remainder of the image was masked and the sky was given an even graduation of exposure—or burned-in—so as to present a gradual transition from black to light gray. [74]

Volume five presented the Mandan, Arikara, and Atsina or Gros Ventre tribes. ''In the present weakened condition of the Mandan tribe,'' Curtis wrote in his introduction, ''there is scant material for illustration.''[76] Nevertheless he did succeed in making photographs of the Mandans' sacred Turtle drums, which according to Mandan beliefs were not to be seen by White people, much less photographed.[77] The account of the incident which Curtis offered—probably years later—described how he had arranged through his interpreter, A. B. Upshaw, to pay the unscrupulous keeper of the drums $500 for the privilege of photographing them.[100] This account also included a swashbuckling tale: Curtis had to trudge through a raging blizzard to reach the cabin of the Turtles' keeper, where he was then forced to take a cleansing sweat bath before seeing the drums. In light of the methods Curtis used to photograph the Navajo Yebechai dance, it is plausible that Curtis did pay for the opportunity to photograph the Mandan Turtles. The story about the blizzard, however, was probably a bit of retrospective embroidery on Curtis's part since he photographed the Turtles during the summer of 1908.[101]

Curtis's photographs of the Arikara are devoted primarily to performances of ceremonies staged for his benefit.[102] His photographs of the Atsina again allude to military activities with images such as *War-Party's Farewell* and *On the War-Path*.[78–79]

Published in 1911 and devoted to the Piegan, Cheyenne, and

[66] Edward Curtis with Custer Scouts at the Custer Monument
Edward Curtis

Curtis spent a great deal of time retracing the events of Custer's last attempt to exterminate Indians. He is depicted here posing with some of the Crow Indian scouts who worked for Custer.

Arapaho, volume six was the last to deal with the Plains tribes until volume eighteen was published seventeen years later. In his introduction Curtis deferred to other authorities. ''The Piegan myths and folk-tales have been so fully treated by Dr. George Bird Grinnell and Dr. Clark Wissler that it seems hardly advisable to record them again.'' In a similar manner, he bowed to the research on the Arapaho of Drs. A. L. Kroeber and George A. Dorsey, saying that space in *The North American Indian* might more usefully be devoted to other topics. Military activities again figured prominently in his description of the Cheyenne:

[text continued on page 104]

[67] UPSHAW—APSAROKE
Edward Curtis

A. B. Upshaw, a Crow Indian, worked for Curtis as an interpreter. For this portrait he wore a costume so as to appear ''Indian'' to Curtis's viewers.

[68] A. B. UPSHAW—
       INTERPRETER
       Credited to F. A. Rinehart

Curtis's lab technician, Adolph Muhr, had
worked previously for Omaha photographer
F. A. Rinehart. Muhr actually took most of
the pictures (probably including this one)
for which Rinehart later became famous.
This portrait, made about seven years
before Curtis's photograph, shows Upshaw
as he ordinarily appeared.

[69]

X2473

[69] LITTLE DOG (SHUNKALA)
[70] SITTING OWL—HITDATSA
   Edward Curtis

Although the subjects of these portraits are from different tribes, Curtis photographed them in the same costume. The costume was probably a prop, which Curtis carried with him to make his subjects look ''Indian.''

[71] APSAROKE WAR GROUP
Edward Curtis

This image is another monumental allusion to military activities that its subjects no longer practiced. Its bold composition is yet another example of Curtis's skill at pictorial photography.

[72] READY FOR THE CHARGE—APSAROKE
Edward Curtis

Curtis was particularly interested in the Crow, or Apsaroke, Indians. The extremely low camera angle dramatizes what Curtis thought was the "superiority" of the Crow as warriors. The impression that the subject towers above the viewer is accentuated by the way the image was cropped inward from the sides.

98

[73]   X2813-08

[73] CRYING TO THE SPIRITS
(before burning-in)

[74] CRYING TO THE SPIRITS
(after burning-in)

Edward Curtis

This image is shot from downhill of the subject so that he appears to stand above the viewer. To increase the dramatic effect of this photograph, Curtis had the sky burned-in in the darkroom. Instead of appearing white, as it does in the unmanipulated image, the sky displays a gradual darkening of tones.

[75] RIGID AND STATUESQUE
Edward Curtis

Both this image and its title indicate Curtis's concern for drama and romance in his portrayal of Indians. This concern has given Curtis's photographs much of their artistic strength and popular appeal. It was also, however, the primary cause of Curtis's failure to portray his subjects as they actually looked.

[76] THE BATHER—MANDAN
Edward Curtis

Curtis complained of ''scant material for illustration'' among the Mandan tribe. In this image he made use of the simplest costume available. Something along the horizon was also retouched away, perhaps a wagon or an automobile.

[77] THE SACRED TURTLES—MANDAN
Edward Curtis

According to a story which Curtis related years later, the Mandan believed that White people should not see these turtle effigy drums—much less photograph them. Also, according to Curtis, he paid an unscrupulous medicine man $500 to be allowed to make this photograph.

[78]

[78] WAR-PARTY'S FAREWELL—ATSINA

[79] ON THE WAR-PATH—ATSINA

Edward Curtis

These two reenactments posed for Curtis's camera repeat his preoccupation with what most of the public believed was an inherent tendency among Indians toward "hostility."

The story of their tribal existence since coming in contact with Caucasians shows an unequalled struggle against inevitable subjection. Their activities were such that for eighteen years the reports of the Office of Indian Affairs, the army records, and the general press teemed with reports of their hostilities.[103]

Noticeably less extreme than his references to the military behavior of other tribes, these remarks mark the start of a moderation—however incomplete—in Curtis's attitudes. The main body of the text, although probably not written by him, makes frequent mention of vicious behavior on the part of Whites.

Strictly speaking, the Piegan were never at war with the United States. The attack on Red Horn's camp in January, 1870, in which one hundred and seventy-three (three-fourths of whom were women and children) were massacred, was officially only a "killing." Had the incident been reversed and Red Horn and his people made an early morning attack on a Montana village of three hundred inhabitants and killed one hundred and seventy-three of them, regardless of sex or age, every member of the attacking party who could have been caught would have been hanged on the spot.[104]

   This moderation in the text did not reflect a corresponding change in Curtis's general approach to his photography. In the romantic pictorial *At the Water's Edge,* the diagonal swirl of the water line and the reflections of two lodges in the water are given vastly greater importance than the lodges themselves.[80] Had the purpose of this image been documentary rather than pictorial, the lodges might have been allowed more than the one-sixth of the frame which they actually fill. Again, *Cheyenne Warriors* (probably the image James Mooney had objected to) is presented for

[80] AT THE WATER'S EDGE—PIEGAN
Edward Curtis

This image makes it clear that Curtis was more concerned with documenting a feeling than with documenting events or objects. The reflections of two lodges and the dramatic diagonal swirl of the water line fill a much greater part of this romantic pictorial than do the lodges themselves. Once again the composition, which gives Curtis's images their artistic power, detracted from the usefulness of the images as scientific documents.

[81] C H E Y E N N E   W A R R I O R S
Edward Curtis

James Mooney, an anthropologist who was unusually enlightened for his time, objected to Curtis's use of the term "warrior" to describe Indians. Mooney thought such a label was inaccurate for describing people who were not engaging in war. Although Curtis respected Mooney, he continued, nevertheless, to use the term "warrior" frequently.

[82]

[82] IN A PIEGAN LODGE (before retouching)

[83] IN A PIEGAN LODGE (after retouching)

Edward Curtis

In the original negative of this image an object in a box—perhaps a medal or a clock—appeared between the two men depicted. By the time the image had been printed as a gravure in *The North American Indian*, the object had been retouched away.

108

[84] WISHHAM GIRL

[85] WISHHAM GIRL PROFILE

Edward Curtis

Among Curtis's tribal "types," these two
portraits are unusual in that they conform closely
to standards in anthropometric photography. As
Curtis pointed out, the "headdress" included
coins which had come from China.

[84]

pictorial effect: the riders are depicted above a staccato diagonal of grass, from a low camera angle, and with their backs to the camera. The tones of the sky descend in a diagonal so perfectly the inverse of that of the grass as to suggest they were achieved through burning-in, with the clouds the result of retouching.[81] *In a Piegan Lodge,* a work more oriented toward documentation, is nevertheless missing what appears to have been a medal or an alarm clock which was retouched out of the original image.[82–83]

In 1910 Curtis returned to the Northwest to complete his work on volumes seven and eight, which dealt with the tribes of the northwestern interior, and to begin work on volumes nine through eleven, which were to cover the tribes of the northwest coast.

Volumes seven and eight, both published in 1911, show a marked increase in Curtis's use of the anthropometrical format of frontal and profile portraits, titled as "Types" of a tribe.[84–87] Both volumes include the usual complement of romantic pictorials whose documentary usefulness is dubious. *On Nespilim Creek, Nespilim Girl,* and *In the Forest—Cayuse* are strikingly similar in composition and costume. Again, although it is difficult to tell with certainty, it seems that the dress and hat appearing in these images were Curtis's props. These photographs are also examples of a common dichotomy existing between Curtis's pictorials of men and those of women. Conforming to traditions in pictorialist photography, Curtis tended to show men involved in activities— as warriors, medicine men, or hunters. He frequently showed women as inactive, presenting them merely as aesthetic objects— girls, maids, or maidens.[88–90] While this sexism can perhaps be understood as a symbolic attitude of the time, it is yet another dimension of the sacrifice of ethnographic accuracy in the interest of pictorial aesthetics.[91] This is particularly ironic in light of frequent references in the text to the slightness of difference between Indian men and women:

Physically the women are equal to any task, however hard. Observed at work, they seem even stronger than the men. In civilization many gener- ations of safeguarding and protecting women have created what we term the "weaker sex"; but among the hunting tribes especially the life of the women has been such as to develop the greatest physical strength, resulting in slight differentiation in features or in endurance of the sexes.[105]

[85]

[86]

[87]

[86] YELLOW BULL—NEZ PERCE

[87] NEZ PERCE WARRIOR

    Edward Curtis

Although these portraits are of different subjects, the Nez Perce men appear to be wearing the same bonnet. Again, the bonnet may have been a prop, which Curtis carried with him to help create the illusion of "Indianness."

[88]   [89]   [90]

[88] NESPILIM GIRL
[89] THE CHIEF HAD A BEAUTIFUL DAUGHTER
[90] THE HOPI MAIDEN

Edward Curtis

In his romantic pictorials, Curtis often portrayed women as inactive aesthetic objects. Whereas women were described as ''girls'' or ''maidens,'' men were portrayed as ''warriors'' or ''scouts.'' Sexism was typical of pictorial photography in Curtis's time, but it affected the usefulness of his photographs as ethnographic documents.

[91] AT THE TRYSTING PLACE
Edward Curtis

This subtle allusion to White myths about the sexuality of Indian women
does not go as far as Case & Draper's photographs, which frequently
included nudity. (See image 35.)

BUSINESS ENERGY AND PERSEVERANCE

By 1911, according to Curtis's original five-year plan, all twenty volumes and accompanying portfolios of *The North American Indian* were to have been completed. As it was, Curtis had already required by 1909 the infusion of an additional loan from J. P. Morgan, above his earnings from sales of subscriptions to his series. Sales of *The North American Indian* had gone well until 1907, but thereafter had slowed considerably. Rather than attributing this slowness to a slackening in popular interest following the fanfare accompanying the beginning of the series, Curtis blamed his sluggish sales on the worldwide economic depression that had begun in 1907.[106] The corporation formed to handle publication of *The North American Indian* had continued in its dedicated efforts to sell the work, but with only minor success. In 1910 a European sales representative—referred to by Curtis as "the noble appearing English animal named Bell"—had simply disappeared, taking with him only a small amount of capital, but leaving his obligations for sales unfulfilled. As Curtis wrote to F. W. Hodge, "This is a serious matter with me, as I had expected him to make an active selling campaign. I will have to work all the harder during the coming winter to make up for his failure."[107]

Curtis had mortgaged virtually everything he owned. Facing bankruptcy—of both himself and his corporation—he was forced to terminate work on *The North American Indian* for the winters of 1910–11 and 1911–12 and to devote himself full time to fundraising.

Without money, but certainly not without means, Curtis was no neophyte to the world of fundraising. Had he been able to hire representatives whose abilities in public relations matched his own, Curtis would have found *The North American Indian* a vastly simpler undertaking. Even his phenomenal "business energy," however, was seriously taxed by the financial plight in which his project had become mired.

Curtis was an experienced lecturer. Resorting to the media skills honed in the days prior to his loans from Morgan, Curtis went on the road with an extravaganza, which he referred to privately as his "entertainment." Billed variously as the *Curtis Indian Picture Opera* and *The Curtis Picture Musicale,* the entertainment was an innovative multimedia presentation. Narrated by Curtis, it included the projection of both hand-tinted lantern slides and motion pictures. It also included musical accompaniment scored by the Boston composer Henry F. Gilbert from Curtis's wax cylinder recordings of Indian music, and played by a full twenty-two piece orchestra.

In November 1911 the entertainment played to a capacity audience at Carnegie Hall in New York City. "The enthusiasm," Curtis wrote to his friend Edmund S. Meany, "was quite out of the ordinary. . . . It was certainly a tribute to the work and unto myself, which should make anyone very happy." While in New York, Curtis also performed at the Brooklyn Institute, where a man he described as "Professor Hooper" told him:

I was the first to ever give them what he considered the real Indian; and he continued to say that he thought the entertainment a message of more than national importance; that it should be heard in every town in the United States, not only by the adults in the evening but in the afternoon so that the school children could see and hear: and he further said that "I feel this so strongly that I shall state it in my address before the Academy of Science at its annual meeting in Washington.[108]

The description of the entertainment which Curtis gave Meany, however, was not entirely so positive:

I passed through seventeen kinds of hell in getting this thing under way, and I will say to you that I do not believe anyone else would have held on as I have this winter. I kept the thing going under unfortunate New England bookings where our average daily loss was to exceed $300.00. . . . We are now through with the unfortunate bookings of a stupid agency and are working in our own way with my own advance men, and will accept no bookings in unimportant towns, and only under auspices where they can fill the largest auditorium at regular theatre prices.[109]

By January 1912 the success which Curtis had foreseen had failed to materialize. Sustaining heavy losses, the entertainment, like *The North American Indian,* had gone into debt. The reminder of its tour was cancelled, and it was all Curtis could do to raise the funds to pay off its outstanding bills.[110]

Curtis evidently attempted to revive the entertainment the following winter, as it showed at Seattle's Metropolitan Theater in December 1912.[111] But again it failed to become the sustaining source of funds for *The North American Indian* which Curtis had hoped it would be.

Curtis and his staff—which, strangely, appears to have expanded while he was preoccupied with finances—had continued to work on the tribes of the Northwest Coast. During most of the two years between publication of volumes eight and nine, Curtis had devoted his energies to the ill-fated entertainment. Two years after his projected completion date, Curtis, struggling under a virtual absence of funds, had published less than half of the promised twenty volumes of *The North American Indian.* In March 1913 he wrote to Bella de Costa Greene at the House of Morgan, describing his financial woes and explaining that he feared his project was nearing an untimely end. He expressed a desire to meet with her at the end of April to discuss his work. As if to put the finishing touches on Curtis's feelings of desperation, J. P. Morgan died, throwing hopes for further financial assistance into extreme doubt.

Shortly thereafter volume nine was published with a tribute, "In Memory of Mr. J. Pierpont Morgan," bound in as a preface. Written by Curtis and dated April 16, 1913, it began: "In the final hour of producing this volume we are saddened and borne down with the loss of the patron who made the work in its full scope possible." The tribute continued with a confidence unrepresentative of Curtis's private description of his feelings: "It is true the undertaking has required the cooperation of many others, yet the confidence manifested by Mr. Morgan at the outset resulted in subsequent support which has aided so greatly in bringing the work to a stage that makes its completion assured." Given the disastrous state of *The North American Indian's* finances, this tribute also had the ring of a thinly-veiled fundraising appeal when it stated that

the purchase of a picture or book already produced is but a change of ownership. To make possible the production of an important picture or book is an actual addition to the sum of human knowledge and a forward step in the development of the race.[112]

By appealing to his readers' desire for "development of the race," Curtis perhaps hoped to stimulate their generosity. More specifically, Curtis seems to have been promoting the good will of Morgan's son, Jack, in hopes that the family would assume the elder Morgan's patronage. On April 22, 1913, Curtis wrote again to Bella de Costa Greene. Claiming that he was making no appeal to Jack Morgan, he did ask Greene to put in a good word for his work, should Mr. Morgan ask about it. Jack Morgan ultimately decided to continue his family's financial assistance to *The North American Indian.* Curtis was able, though only briefly, to breathe a sigh of relief.

During this period of intense financial worry Curtis evolved yet another inventive—and costly—scheme for raising funds. Beginning as far back as 1910 he and his staff had been working on a silent movie. The film might be thought of in retrospect as a prototype of the ethnographic docu-drama. Set among the Kwakiutl tribe of the Northwest Coast, the plot was replete with romance and violence. The story was derived from Curtis's study of the Kwakiutl and from information provided by a Kwakiutl informant named George Hunt, a previous employee of the well-known anthropologist, Franz Boas. While it utilized material from Kwakiutl legends and oral history, the movie was arranged to hold the attention of its audience through calculated development of dramatic suspense. The Kwakiutl actors were directed by Curtis and wore costumes commissioned for the film.

In the Land of the Headhunters, as the film was titled, was released in 1914. Its anticipated popular success failed to materialize, and the film closed almost immediately—like the entertainment, yet another financial loss. Curtis's effort at filmmaking, however, was not without historical importance. Robert Flaherty found *In the Land of the Headhunters* an important influence in the making of his classic ethnographic film, *Nanook of the North.*[113]

MORE *PICTURESQUE*
INDIANS

Though often overlapping the progress of the film, work on *The North American Indian* had nevertheless continued. Volume nine had covered the Salishan tribes of the coast—the Chimakum and the Quilliute. The photographs for this volume were similar to those of volume seven in that they show the influence of anthropometric portraiture. Interestingly, the accompanying portfolio included the nonethnographic pictorials *The Clam Digger, Evening on the Sound* (now titled *Evening on Puget Sound*), and *Homeward*. Curtis had won first prize in the genre category at the 1898 convention of the Photographers Association of America for these images long before he had conceived of becoming an ethnographic photographer.

Although he titled his film about the Kwakiutl *In the Land of the Headhunters,* Curtis wrote of the Northwest Coast tribes in his introduction to volume nine:

Their mental inferiority to the more picturesque tribes of the Plains has been considerably exaggerated by many observers; they were far above the stage of savagery, and their development was well suited to meet the peculiar demands of their environment.[114]

Volume ten, published in 1915, one year after *In the Land of the Headhunters,* seems almost a companionpiece to the film. Many of the images are pictorials of activities included in the plot of the film and appear actually to have been made at the same time.[92–94]

In his introduction to the volume, Curtis confidently stated that "the primitive garments shown in the illustrations were prepared by Kwakiutl men and women for the author, and are correct in all respects." He hedged with the statement that "such costumes, of course, are not now in use." Curtis also credits the efforts of his informant, George Hunt, and refers to the work of Franz Boas, "The Social Organization of the Kwakiutl Indians," as having "greatly simplified" his work on the volume. In her book, written with Victor Boesen, Curtis's daughter, Florence Graybill, refers to Boas as having tried in 1907 to discredit Curtis's work.[115] In fact Curtis appears neither to have liked nor entirely to have trusted Boas.[116] Although generous enough to credit Boas's work, he neglected to point out that George Hunt had received his ethnographic training while working for Boas. The final sentence of the introduction to volume ten notes the sudden death of Curtis's trusted darkroom assistant, Adolf F. Muhr, whose efforts in darkroom manipulation had been a central pillar in Curtis's work.

Published in 1916, volume eleven presented the Nootka and Haida tribes, with the text focusing largely on the history of Nootka relations with Whites. The illustrations are meager in comparison with others taken both before and after this volume. A great number of them are of totem poles, and although they are somewhat repetitious from an artistic standpoint, they are among the least manipulated—and therefore perhaps the most documentarily sound—of Curtis's images. The portraits, however, do not represent a significant departure from his earlier work: he used wigs to conceal the short hair of his subjects,[117] and he may also have reused the costumes made for *In the Land of the Headhunters*.

During the period when Curtis and his staff were working on volumes ten and eleven, they were continually, despite Jack Morgan's willingness to make further loans available, beset with financial concerns. H. H. Sheets, a fundraiser working out of *The North American Indian's* corporate office in New York, had lobbied in Washington to obtain a congressional appropriation for Curtis's work. In a letter to Morgan in 1915, Sheets indicated that a lack of sufficient capital was threatening his chances for success. Morgan regretted that he was not in a position to offer Sheets a loan, and the appropriation was never obtained.[118]

As a further hindrance to the financial health of *The North

[92] MASKED DANCERS—QAGYUHL
Edward Curtis

This plate shows people wearing the costumes that Curtis had made for the actors in his docu-drama about the Kwakiutl Indians. *In the Land of the Headhunters,* as the silent film was called, was released in 1914 but was a box office disaster. The film was, however, an important influence on Robert Flaherty, whose *Nanook of the North* is considered to be a classic ethnographic film.

[93] PASSING A DREADED POINT
Edward Curtis

This dramatic pictorial was probably made during the filming of *In the Land of the Headhunters,* as it depicts a scene from the movie plot.

[94] HOMEWARD
Edward Curtis

Curtis made this image in 1898 and did not originally intend it to be used as an ethnographic document. He decided, however, to include the image in *The North American Indian*.

[95] VANISHING INTO THE MISTS
Dixon & Wanamaker

In 1914 Joseph Dixon published a book called *The Vanishing Race*. The book was illustrated with photographs in a sepia-tone format extremely similar to Curtis's. Curtis believed that these were "fakey imitations" of his work. Although the images published by Dixon lack the graphic strength of Curtis's work, they do share his passion for drama and romance.

American Indian, Rodman Wanamaker, in conjunction with Joseph Dixon, had started in 1913 a project which cut in on Curtis's market. In a series of letters to Hodge, Curtis made continually disparaging remarks about Dixon and Wanamaker's project to photograph Indians, implying that he found it too similar to his own for comfort.[119] Writing to Edmund Meany following the publication of photographs in a book by Dixon, Curtis complained openly of plagiarism and called the images "fakey imitations" of his own.[120]

Curtis's anger would seem justified. Dixon's book had taken the title of the opening gravure, *The Vanishing Race*, from *The North*

American Indian. It presented halftone reproductions—in themselves strikingly similar to Curtis's—in a format so like that of *The North American Indian* that it made Curtis's accusation of imitation seem quite legitimate. The Dixon-Wanamaker images were perhaps even more manipulative of the photographic process and of their subjects than Curtis's were. But they lacked the graphic power of Curtis's images and are now comparatively unknown. [95]

Due to a combination of unfortunate circumstances, 1916 marked the beginning of a six-year hiatus in publication of *The North American Indian*. The death of the darkroom wizard, Adolf Muhr, must seriously have rocked Curtis's confidence in his ability to maintain the standard of image quality so important in establishing his work. His financial situation was still far from comfortable. His personal life was heading for disaster. And in 1918 Curtis's wife, Clara, filed for divorce.[121] During the eighteen years that Curtis had devoted in time and money to *The North American Indian* and ancillary projects, Clara had borne most of the responsibility for raising their family. Apparently the strain of her husband's overwhelming commitment to his work had taken its toll. The divorce, according to his daughter Florence, was immensely painful for Curtis and caused him to suffer from severe bouts of depression.[122]

The North American Indian resurfaced in 1922 with publication of volume twelve on the Hopi. In his introduction Curtis wrote that "further work was done" in 1919, but he also noted that "in collecting and preparing the material for publication I have had the continual collaboration of Mr. W. E. Myers, who has shown an extraordinary devotion to the work." This volume was evidently a compilation of earlier work:

It is most fortunate that a great many of the pictures were obtained so long ago; for, conservative as these people are, there has been a great change in their mode of life, hence many of the photographs here presented could not have been made in more recent years.[123]

Curtis was also at pains to point out that "the copyright dates do not always coincide with the year in which the photographs were made." In fact, there is strong evidence of Adolf Muhr's darkroom technique throughout volume twelve, which would indicate that most and perhaps all of the images dated from Curtis's work with the Hopi between 1900 and 1912. Curtis's new darkroom technician—whose identity remains obscure—printed the images for copyright deposit with a white border, unlike those printed by Muhr. Although there are a few images among those on deposit for volume twelve which have the white border, even these tend to exhibit Muhr's style in negative retouching.

There is one image among these illustrations that explicitly announces itself as a departure from the ethnographic present. *Hopi Farmers, Yesterday and Today* depicts one man in a loin cloth and another wearing a shirt and blue jeans. [96] Although it appears that Curtis's concept of his work, and particularly of the ethnographic present, was undergoing a gradual change during the 1920s, this image is copyrighted, enigmatically, in 1906. While later copyrights might have been for earlier images, this image had to have been made before it was copyrighted.

The remainder of the images accompanying this volume tend to reflect the normal style of Curtis's early approach. Attracted perhaps by a novel hairstyle (''Atoo''), he included a large number of highly posed pictorial portraits of his idea of femininity. [97] There is also a heavy pictorial emphasis on the Hopi Snake Dance. [98–99]

Referring to the "subtle charm" of the Hopi, Curtis wrote that "this was especially so in earlier years, when their manner of life indicated comparatively slight contact with civilization." In regard to the Snake Dance, Curtis must have been comparing the dance he had previously observed with the situation at the time he was writing. As Curtis well knew, the Snake Dance had already become a heavy attraction for tourists in the Southwest by the time he first visited the Hopi in 1900. Photographs of the Snake Dance from the 1890s show large numbers of tourists, frequently with photographers among them. [100–103]

George Wharton James, writing in *Camera Craft* in 1902—four years before most of Curtis's images of the Snake Dance were made—described the regulations for viewing the dance:

. . . it was decided that the photographers present—and they were legion—must be kept within a certain line, and that no one without a camera would be permitted in their preserves. This was an innovation. Hitherto every man had chosen his own field, and moved to and fro wherever he liked—in front of his neighbor or someone else; kicking down another fellow's tripod and sticking his elbow in the next fellow's lens. . . .

This placing of restrictions on photographers will undoubtedly continue

[96] HOPI FARMERS, YESTERDAY AND TODAY
Edward Curtis

This image is extremely unusual among Curtis's early photographs in that it makes explicit visual reference to the changes that had taken place among the Hopi during the time since they had come into contact with Whites.

as the dance becomes better known and attracts more people. Each year the number who flock there is greater, and it is imperative that some regulations be laid down or the poor Indians would be run over in the eager desire of the visitors to see them handle the deadly reptiles.[124]

In the same article James further described how the presence of so many photographers had led to changes in the ceremony. Originally the ceremony had included the drinking of an emetic by

120

X1966-00

[97] WALPAI MAIDENS
Edward Curtis

Curtis was fascinated by the "Atoo" hairstyle
worn by the women in this pictorial.

[98] SHIPAULOVI SNAKE DANCE

[99] SNAKE DANCERS ENTERING THE PLAZA

Edward Curtis

In these two images of the Hopi Snake Dance, Curtis used a very large aperture, or lens opening, so that the tourists in the background appear only as indistinct blurs.

[100] SNAKE DANCE AT
HUALPI, MOQUI
INDIAN VILLAGE,
ARIZONA, 1897
Ben Wittick

As early as the mid-1890s, the Hopi
Snake Dance had become a major
tourist attraction. Several
photographers are clearly visible among
the spectators in this photograph.

[101] MOKI SNAKE DANCE AT ORAIBI, 1897
E. H. Maude

In this photograph, taken three years before Curtis went to the Southwest for the first time, a White photographer stands practically in line with the Hopi Antelope priests.

[102] Snake Kiva Exterior
Photographer unknown

As early as 1901 the tourists had become such a nuisance at the Snake Dance that the Hopi felt obliged to put this sign on the Snake Kiva. "To all visitors: the men of the Snake Order desire that none enter the Snake Kiva and that all refrain from making noise in the vicinity thereof."

[103] ANTELOPE MEN IN LINE. MOKI SNAKE DANCE, ORAIBI, 1896
George Wharton James

George Wharton James was among the earlier photographers at the Snake Dance. In an article in *Camera Craft* in 1902, James called attention to the fact that tourism had caused changes in the Snake Dance ceremonies. Early in his own career, Curtis had encouraged and profited from the tourist trade in the Southwest.

the Snake priests, who then vomited together in full public view. As James explained, they had later taken to drinking the emetic in private, so as to escape the prurient eye of the camera. He predicted that "it will not be long before one can write a learned and accurate paper from the standpoint of the scientific ethnology on 'the change in religious ceremonies owing to the camera.'"

Curtis, far from his stated desire to document those aspects rapidly disappearing from Indian cultures, did not publish photographs of the drinking of the emetic. Displaying his ethnocentrism, he wrote to Hodge in 1924 that in the Southwest

there are many ceremonies and parts of ceremonies which are decidedly of the obscene type. As we all know, education and contact with civilization has a strong tendency to eliminate such ceremonies. Unfortunately Collier [later the Commissioner of Indian Affairs], in his complete ignorance of the subject and desiring some popular angle of the Indian subject to which he can draw support, has done much to encourage the revival of the most objectionable ceremonies.[125]

Under John Collier's administration during the New Deal, the Bureau of Indian Affairs engaged in a progressive program of applied anthropology, and among Whites of his time Collier was surprisingly free of ethnocentric prejudice.

Of the photographs which Curtis did take of the Snake Dance, many are heavily retouched. In those where tourists might otherwise have been visible in the background, Curtis used a very large lens opening to shorten his range of focus so that the observers appear only as indistinct blurs.

Volumes thirteen through fifteen, published between 1924 and 1926, covered the few survivors of the many tribes of California and southern Oregon. When he reemerged from his long absence from "the field" in 1922, Curtis had changed his approach to his work. He referred privately to his work in California as "Gathering Up the Fragments."[126] Curtis now traveled in a car (which he called a "French Lizzie") to find many of his subjects, who were by this time migrant farm workers or laborers of other sorts in the White economy. The Indians of California, to an extent unequaled elsewhere, had been the victims of genocide and disease. As Curtis himself wrote:

All Indians suffered through the selfishness of our own race, but the natives of California were the greatest sufferers of all. They were not warlike. They consisted of small, isolated groups lacking the social instinct and the strength of self-defense against a force so strong as ours.

By what was supposed to have been a treaty they signed away their lands, in lieu of which they were to be granted definite areas much smaller in extent, together with certain goods and chattels, and educational advantages. This treaty was never ratified, yet we took advantage of one of its proposed provisions by assuming immediate possession of the Indian lands, by which cunning the majority of the natives were left homeless. . . . The conditions are still so acute that, after spending many months among these scattered groups of Indians, the Author finds it difficult even to mention the subject with calmness.[127]

Ironically, calmness pervades Curtis's photographs of the California Indians. His attitudes about "Indianness" appear to have softened considerably by this point. Although he referred to the lack of a "Social instinct," equating the California Indians with species evolutionarily retarded, he also more frequently recognized differences as cultural rather than racial.[128] This softening of attitudes allowed Curtis to make portraits of men with short hair wearing manufactured clothing, and pictorials of modern houses built with milled lumber. [104–105] It did not, however, prevent him from having many of his subjects strip, and, donning loin cloths or other costumes, pose for pictorials alluding to "primitiveness." [106–110] The long hair in many of his photographs of men was probably a wig worn at Curtis's request. Even in those portraits showing men with short hair and modern clothing, Curtis used such a large lens opening that often only the tip of his subject's nose was in focus—thereby obscuring the hair and dress.

Volumes sixteen and seventeen, both published in 1926, returned to the Pueblo tribes of the Southwest. Like volume twelve on the Hopi, most of the images in these volumes date from Curtis's work in the first decade of the century. [111–113] Reverting again to a somewhat qualified ethnocentrism, Curtis wrote in his introduction to volume sixteen that

the right to maintain esoteric organizations and to exclude aliens from knowledge of religious ceremonies can not be questioned, but from the viewpoint of civilization it is regrettable that the priestly dominance of the populations is such as to oppose progress on the part of the younger generation. . . .[129]

This statement also seems ironic, since the text—though probably written by his assistant, William Myers—decries the damaging effects of "civilization" in the form of tourism, which Curtis himself had helped to stimulate in the Southwest:

Isleta, twelve miles from the largest town in New Mexico, a station on the transcontinental railway, skirted by an automobile highway, beset by tourists whose vehicles thread their narrow, haphazard streets to the imminent peril of toddling infants and frightened fowls and whirl past the kiva to the undoubtedly intense annoyance of the priests, one expects to find so altered by all these contacts as to hold little of interest to the investigator.[130]

The introduction to volume seventeen begins with an acknowledgment of the suffering that early contact with Whites brought to the Pueblo Indians. But Curtis suddenly lurched back into stereotype when instead of recognizing the Pueblo Revolt of 1680 as an attempt by Indians to cast off their oppression by Spanish missionaries, he wrote that the Indians "avenged the interference with their traditions by missionaries by instigating the rebellion and visiting death, with typical savage brutality, on every Spanish missionary whom they could seize."[131]

Curtis admitted that both these volumes on the Pueblos had been founded on "admittedly incomplete data." [114] The photographs also seem less graphically powerful than those accompanying other volumes, and it appears that Curtis was again "gathering up the fragments."

Published in 1928, volume eighteen, covering the Chipewyan, Cree, and Sarsi, appears again to be compiled from earlier work. Although almost all the photographs are copyrighted in 1926, there is no indication by Curtis of when they were taken. Some photographs may have been shot in 1925, but it seems probable that many were from a considerably earlier period.

In the introduction, Curtis shows no sign of increased enlightenment about racism and ethnocentrism:

Intimate contact with fur-traders, who because of the allegedly superior charms of the Cree women commonly chose their wives among them, apparently had no beneficial effect on the tribal descendants, for the modern Cree of Alberta are decidedly inferior both in physique and in observance of the laws of hygiene.[132]

Curtis was still enamored of his old belief in racial and tribal hierarchy. The photographs chosen to illustrate volume eighteen provide considerable evidence of many of the manipulations characterizing his early work. His posed portrait *A Cree* depicts a man with a sullen expression whose glazed stare seems to confirm Curtis's opinion of the tribe. *Berry Pickers in Camp—Chipewyan* shows the cradleboard appearing in *Isqe-Sis ("Woman Small")*

and Child—Cree, which would imply that it was a prop used without reference to tribal identity. [115–116] And *The Moose Hunter—Cree* is merely a tighter framing of exactly the same pose used in *Calling a Moose—Cree.* [117–118]

Oklahoma: Trying to Get What Doesn't Exist

A strange aberration among the volumes of *The North American Indian,* volume nineteen is an attempt to fill out the twenty volumes promised to the subscribers to the series. In it Curtis sets out to account for the cultural nightmare that had resulted from the forced concentration of Indian populations in what had once been the "Indian Territory" of Oklahoma. Curtis had lost the services of his dedicated assistant, William Myers,[133] and was working with a new assistant whom his editor, F. W. Hodge, had recommended. Later Hodge determined that the new assistant was not sufficiently competent.[134] Perhaps at Hodge's suggestion, Curtis took a greater responsibility for the researching and writing of the text of volume nineteen than he had taken on any volume since the first of the series. In his correspondence with Hodge during work on this volume, Curtis was often embroiled in argument. "You say," he wrote, " 'Tribes, for example, which have not been influenced by Christianity.' There ain't no such animal." In another example from the same correspondence, " 'Wichita theology.' You seemingly object to the use of the word other than associated with Christian religion. I see nothing in Webster to indicate that Christianity has the exclusive use of the word."[135] What is interesting about these points is that Curtis is arguing against ethnocentrism and the use of the ethnographic present. Again he wrote to Hodge:

You say the Comanche material is inadequate. I grant you that it does not make a strong showing, but one cannot make something from nothing. We covered the ground with the most intelligent of the present day educated man as interpreter and helper. With his help, we talked with all of the old men of the tribe. Day by day we struggled to get what we thought should exist. Finally, our interpreter, Mr. Tebo, turned to me in some exasperation and stated: "You are trying to get what does not exist." The only material we could find was countless, meaningless, fragmentary obscene stories of the camp-fire type; no point to them beyond the obscenity.[136]

Probably because of problems such as that just described, Curtis devoted most of the text of volume nineteen to histories of the

[text continued on page 137]

[104] A MAIDU MAN
Edward Curtis

Most of the Indians in California who had survived extermination during the nineteenth century had become agricultural workers, or had become integrated in other ways into the White economy by the time Curtis started photographing them. This portrait displays an increased willingness by Curtis to show his subjects without dressing them in costumes. He still, however, used such a large lens opening that most of the image is not in focus.

[105] MODERN HUPA HOME
Edward Curtis

Like *A Maidu Man*, this photograph indicates that Curtis recognized that his subjects in California no longer lived as they had before contact with Whites.

[106] SPEARING SALMON
Edward Curtis

Even though Curtis had chosen not to costume some of his subjects in California, this choice was far from absolute. The subject of this pleasantly composed pictorial was probably wearing a wig, along with an extremely simple costume.

[107] RATTLESNAKE DESIGN
IN YOKUTS BASKETRY
Edward Curtis

More than half of the frame in this image is
devoted to the depiction of reeds, water,
and rocks. While the texture of the reeds in
the background makes this a very appealing
pictorial, it contributes little to the
documentary significance of the photograph.

[108] FISHING CAMP—LAKE POMO
Edward Curtis

The composition of this photograph makes it a powerfully beautiful image. Curtis explained in his caption that Tule reed huts, such as that depicted, were no longer used by the Pomo, and that he had had this one ''built especially for the occasion.'' One suspects that Curtis planned the placement of the hut more in the interest of pictorial composition than for documentary accuracy.

[109] ON THE SHORES OF CLEAR LAKE
Edward Curtis

In this dramatic pictorial there is no obvious ethnographic significance. The subject was probably wearing a wig and was dressed in the simple costume of a breechclout. He appears to have been posed in a posture of fear, but neither the image nor the caption makes clear what he was supposed to be frightened of.

[110] SHORES OF WALKER LAKE
Edward Curtis

In his caption for this image Curtis explained that at Walker Lake fish "were taken on bone hooks, with double-pointed spears, and in gill-nets." He did not identify the tribe of his subject, and the image itself gives little information about methods of fishing. The repetition of diagonals in Curtis's composition, however, makes it a graphically strong pictorial.

132

[111] POVI-TAMU ("FLOWER MORNING")—SAN
      ILDEFONSO

[112] THE FRUIT GATHERER—SAN ILDEFONSO

[113] GIRL AND JAR—SAN ILDEFONSO

Edward Curtis

Curtis wrote in the caption to his portrait *Flower Morning* that "the
regular features of the comely Morning Flower are not exceptional, for
most Tewa girls, and indeed most Pueblo girls, are not without
attractiveness." Because of her "attractiveness," however, Curtis posed
her again as the subject of *The Fruit Gatherer* and of *Girl and Jar*.

[111]

[112]

[113]

[114] A ZUNI GOVERNOR
Edward Curtis

Although copyrighted in 1925, this image, like *Flower Morning,* was
probably taken in 1905. In his caption Curtis wrote that "this portrait
may well be taken as representative of the typical Pueblo physiognomy."
Though it is used today without scientific pretension, "physiognomy"
was the title of a nineteenth-century pseudoscience that attempted to link
facial characteristics to behavioral tendencies.

[115]

[116]

[115] BERRY PICKERS IN CAMP—CHIPEWYAN

[116] ISQE-SIS ("WOMAN SMALL") AND CHILD—CREE

Edward Curtis

Although the subjects of these two images are captioned as being from different tribes, the same cradleboard appears in both images. Either Curtis misidentified the tribes in question, or the cradleboard was another of his props.

[117]

[118]

[117] THE MOOSE HUNTER—CREE
[118] CALLING A MOOSE—CREE

Edward Curtis

The Moose Hunter was a portfolio plate from volume eighteen of *The North American Indian*, whereas *Calling a Moose* was a text illustration for the volume itself. The former is only a tighter framing of almost exactly the same pose used in the latter.

tribes covered and concentrated particularly on the experiences which brought them to Oklahoma. Although the volume does include periodic reversion to simplistic or ethnocentric explanations of events, these are seldom as extreme as in previous volumes. Had Curtis been confronted with the situation in Oklahoma earlier in his career, one cannot help but wonder how it would have affected his work.

Like the text, the illustrations to volume nineteen diverge conspicuously from others in *The North American Indian*. Though devotees of pictorialism may find them less interesting than some of Curtis's earlier work, these illustrations have vastly greater integrity as ethnographic documents. [119–123] There are occasional retreats to artifice, such as the use of a feather bonnet as a prop. [124–125] But there are also a great number of straightforward portraits of people in their normal dress of the time. Although many of the subjects were posed, still they appear to have had more say about their presentation before the camera so that the resulting images are much closer to the ideal of cooperation between photographer and subject which we think of in contemporary documentary photography.

The final volume of *The North American Indian*, published in 1930, more than thirty years after Curtis had first embarked on his life's work, covered the various tribes of Alaska and the islands in the Bering Sea. Because of their geographical obscurity, these people had been less affected by contact with Whites than the tribes in the states to the south. Unfortunately, therefore, we never really get a chance to see what the effects of Curtis's experiences in Oklahoma were on his view of acculturation. [126] But many of his photographs of houses, water craft, and other material possessions from Alaska are unpretentious documents. [127–129] His portraits, although posed, show more smiling countenances than appear in any, and perhaps all, of the other volumes. Like many of those portraits from Oklahoma, these photographs allow the subjects a decent chance to express themselves as they chose.

Curtis's voyage up the coast of Alaska and into the Bering Sea was extremely arduous. Sailing in a small schooner, he and his crew were tossed about in viciously rough seas, nearly losing their ship and their lives several times. Upon returning to Seattle, Curtis suffered humiliation at the hands of a local judge, who had issued a warrant for his arrest for failure to pay alimony to his ex-wife, Clara.[137] In addition, an old injury in one hip had been aggravated on his trip to Alaska, thus making it difficult for him to walk. Following the failure of the court to produce documents proving a case against him, Curtis limped back to the home he had established in Los Angeles, with both his pride and his body badly battered.

Limping Home

Following publication of volume twenty in 1930, Curtis suffered "a complete physical breakdown."[138] Writing to his old contact from the House of Morgan, Curtis strongly implied that he had become so deeply depressed that he had considered suicide, but had held back and had slowly regained his confidence. A feeling of anti-climax surely followed the completion of an effort as draining and protracted as Curtis's work on *The North American Indian*, so his reaction hardly seems surprising. He had recently been raked over the still smoldering coals of a profoundly painful divorce and was largely without funds after some thirty-four years of "business energy and perseverance." The project had been such an integral part of his life for so many years that it must have been difficult for him to distinguish between them.

Bella de Costa Greene forwarded her letter from Curtis to the still-functioning corporate offices of *The North American Indian*. There it was interpreted by the people handling Curtis's life's work as an appeal for money, and was callously dismissed on the assumption that Curtis was better off than he admitted.

Curtis spent the rest of his life with his daughter Beth and her husband Manford Magnuson in their home in Los Angeles. Much of his time was now devoted to attempts at writing and publishing popular books on Indians and other subjects. While these attempts kept him occupied, none of the books was ever published.

During the last years of Curtis's life his photographs disappeared from public view, except for appearances as incidental illustrations in a few outdated texts. A Boston rare books dealer, The George Lauriat Company, bought the gravure plates and the remaining stock of *The North American Indian*. Attempts to market the remaining sets, however, were not very successful, and by the end of the 1940s, the proposed edition of 500 had ground to a halt with fewer than 300 sets sold. The monument to Edward S. Curtis, which his sales representative had described in 1905, seemed to have toppled on its face, and when Curtis died in 1952, he was virtually unknown.

[119] WILBUR PEEBO—
COMANCHE
Edward Curtis

When faced with the cultural complexities
of Oklahoma in the late 1920s, Curtis finally
began to understand that "the Indian"
whom he had tried to present did not exist.
Although he still occasionally costumed his
subjects, many of his portraits from
Oklahoma are of people as he actually
found them, rather than as he wished them
to be.

[120] THE DANCE—WICHITA
Edward Curtis

The front of an automobile is visible just to the right of center frame in this image. In Curtis's earlier work, the automobile would have been retouched away. In terms of the documentary significance of this photograph, the automobile is useful evidence that helps set the context in which the picture was made.

[121] BUFFALO DANCERS, ANIMAL
       DANCE—CHEYENNE
       Edward Curtis

Although the women depicted in this photograph are
wearing buffalo headgear—perhaps affected at Curtis's
request—they are also wearing their normal clothing.

[122] COMANCHE MOTHERS
Edward Curtis

The four women in this image are holding babies in traditional cradleboards, yet they are wearing dresses of machine-woven and printed fabric. Fence posts are clearly visible, and in the far upper left corner a telephone pole runs down the edge of the frame.

[123] AT THE POOL, ANIMAL DANCE—CHEYENNE
Edward Curtis

The subjects of this photograph are wearing normal clothing of the period. Wagons and parasols, which would have been retouched away in Curtis's earlier work, are easily discernible along the top of the frame.

[124]

[125]

[124] PIPE STEM—OTO

[125] WAKONDA—OTO

Edward Curtis

Since the subjects of these two portraits are wearing the same feather bonnet, it seems that Curtis still used props to make at least some of his subjects look like stereotyped "Indians."

144

[126] KENOWUN—NUNIVAK
Edward Curtis

The last volume of *The North American Indian* was
devoted to the people of Alaska, who had been
influenced much less by White culture than most
Indians in the forty-eight states. It is hard to tell from
the photographs made in Alaska what effect Curtis's
recognition of acculturation in Oklahoma had on his
subsequent work. Many of the portraits from volume
twenty, however, lack the sometimes stilted feeling of
the poses in his earlier work.

[127]

[127] THE VILLAGE—HOOPER BAY
[128] KING ISLAND HOMES
   Edward Curtis

These pictures, although perhaps less aesthetically interesting than much of Curtis's earlier work, are unpretentious and unmanipulative documents of architectural styles.

[128]

KAIAK WITH SEAL HUNTING EQUIPMENT—NUNIVAK
Edward Curtis

The aesthetic arrangement of the objects in this photograph does not detract from the documentation of seal hunting equipment.

BECAUSE THE SITUATION DEMANDS IT

The lapse of *The North American Indian* into obscurity following its completion in 1930 is not reducible to a simple cause. The fact that the nation had plummeted into the depths of the Great Depression was certainly a contributing factor. At a price by that point of $3500 a set, the series was a luxury which few could now afford. Curtis's own personal depression must also have had an effect. His unceasingly aggressive salesmanship had been important to what success *The North American Indian* had enjoyed, and without it the popularity of his work could be expected to diminish. Even as Curtis and the nation struggled out of their respective depressions, attitudes about Indians and "Indianness" were changing. Under the ministrations of Margaret Mead and other progressive thinkers, anthropologists were more inclined to be suspicious of cultural bias and to look at historical ethnography with a critical eye. It is doubtful that changing attitudes among anthropologists had any direct effect on The George Lauriat Company's attempts to sell out the edition of *The North American Indian*. They may, however, have caused some partly conscious hesitation on the part of institutions that might otherwise have bought the series. Popular attitudes about Indians were changing also, but not always in a positive way. Nostalgia about "the vanishing race" had itself mostly disappeared, and Indians, who had not, tended to be viewed according to a variety of disparaging stereotypes. As a result, the potential market for *The North American Indian* among private citizens must certainly have diminished.

The extreme patriotism of the 1950s might have been expected to produce attitudes toward American nativism that would have been beneficial to the popularity of Curtis's work. That patriotism, however, stressed a jingoistic fear of "otherness," which only compounded disrespect for Indians. The program of "termination" embarked on during this period by the federal government was specifically aimed at the centuries-old goal of obliterating what was thought of as cultural Indianness. In the name of the great "melting pot" the government sought to strip Indians of special legal status, hoping to "terminate" their cultural otherness. It is hardly surprising that a tribute to a "vanishing race" would not be terribly popular in a culture which was attempting to "terminate" Indians.

It was probably the civil rights and ecology movements of the 1960s and 1970s that provided the environment in which Curtis's popularity reemerged. Amid the optimistic attitudes about "race relations," which were developing among Whites during this period, attitudes about Indians began to become more positive. But the public still generally accepted the lumping together of diverse cultures. Although the cultural difference between the Kwakiutls and Seminoles, even in the twentieth century, is probably as great as between any two European cultures, the racial stereotype of "the Indian" took on new life. As the ecology movement gained momentum, the stereotype reverted to imagery of "the Noble Savage," who was revered for his "natural simplicity."

It was at approximately this same time that photographs began to gain widespread acceptance as art. Although smaller galleries had put together what were probably the first auctions of photographs during the 1950s, it was not until the 1970s that the big auction houses joined in the movement toward recognition of art-photography.

The emergence of popular interest in photographs as art combined with the simultaneous emergence of "neo-noble-savagism" to produce a tremendous revival in the popular appeal of Curtis's work. In the early 1970s a number of popular books were published presenting reproductions of his photographs. Among the first of these was a monograph—based on a museum exhibition—which juxtaposed Curtis's images with historical quotes from ethnologists and famous Indian figures. These quotes generally enhanced the romantic appeal of Curtis's imagery, but along with the choice of images, the quotes served to obscure the racism and ethnocentrism that were important aspects of his work. This monograph was followed by several other books. Some of these, particularly the two coauthored by Curtis's daughter, Florence

Graybill, tended to follow more closely Curtis's own presentation of his work.

Other museum exhibitions of Curtis's photographs and of photogravures from the portfolios of *The North American Indian* followed close behind, and by the mid-1970s Curtis had become the best known and most popular photographer of Indians in America. Sometime during this meteoric rise to fame, the original gravure plates used to print the photographs for *The North American Indian* were discovered in a Boston warehouse by an enterprising young collector of photographs. By the late 1970s a corporation had been set up to publish heavily edited variations of *The North American Indian*. The gravures in this edition, while printed from the original plates made by John Andrews and Son and by Suffolk Gravure, are slightly different from those in *The North American Indian*. The reason for this is unclear—whether from heavier inking, use of different inks, or whatever other variable in the photogravure printing process—but the results include more obvious evidence of original retouching.

In none of these revivals of Curtis's work has the documentary significance of his photographs been seriously examined. On the contrary, their ethnographic significance is frequently and uncritically reiterated, along with legitimately glowing accounts of their artistic value.

J. C. Warburg, writing in *Camera Work* in 1904, divided photography into three categories: (1) educational and scientific, (2) personal and topographical, and (3) pictorial and artistic.

Roughly speaking, the objects of photography of the first group are the highest attainable accuracy and *truth to fact;* in many cases the minutest details, whether seen by the eye in the original subject or not, are invaluable, and the influence of the personal equation on the result must be reduced to a minimum.

In the third group the ideal is totally different, if not contrary, to that of the first. Here we wish to stimulate the esthetic sensations of the beholder. *Truth to fact* is not wanted, though *truth to appearance* is. The influence of the personal equation is given as full play as possible.[139]

The dichotomy set up by Warburg between "educational and scientific" photography, and "pictorial and artistic" photography corresponds remarkably to the distinction often made between "documentary" and "artistic" in modern photography. In both modern and historical photography, this distinction is somewhat illusory. All art *documents* the subjective perceptions of the artist, and all documents present the *subjective* perceptions of their creators—at least in the selection of what has been documented. In fact, much of what has been presented as documentary photography is highly subjective. The Farm Security Administration (FSA) photographers, whose work was commissioned under Franklin Delano Roosevelt's New Deal, were provided with shooting scripts indicating what in the depression environment to portray, and often even how to portray it.[140] When World War II broke out, most of these photographers transferred to the Office of War Information (OWI). Roy Stryker, who as head of the photographic unit had accompanied them in the move from the FSA to the OWI, instructed them to reverse their orientation. Where previously the photographers had been told to show pictures of depression poverty, they were now informed that they should make images of the proud and productive American worker.[141]

To point out the subjectivity in documentary photographs is not in any way to challenge their importance as documents, but rather to clarify *what kind* of documents they appear to be after close inspection of the evidence surrounding their creation. The photographers working under Roy Stryker at the OWI made stunning documents of an *attitude* that was an immensely powerful aspect of their environment. Similarly, Curtis's photographs of "Indianness" documented an attitude which was important in *his* environment.

The camera never lies. This assertion may seem strange after all the examples just offered of manipulation of the photographic process for dramatic effect. But photographs are not reality (except insofar as they are *real photographs*) and cameras are inanimate objects—they tell lies no more frequently than a printing press or pencil. Writers and photographers can and often *do* lie. "Lying," however, implies an intent to deceive, and only animate, thinking people are capable of harboring such an intent.

When we consider Curtis's photographs as documents, it seems fair to say that he lied, though only infrequently. Occasionally, he intended his viewer to believe that Indians were as he showed them, when in fact he knew this to be false. On the other hand, he made numerous references to things "as they once were," implying that the viewer was being presented with an attempt at historical reconstruction. That he often failed in the attempt has to be taken into account—his documents are only seldom what he presented them as being. But much as Curtis excused George Catlin's mistaken impressions as "only natural," we may often excuse Curtis.

When we consider Curtis's work as art, he must be credited with integrity. Sometimes, as in the case of his tribute to J. P. Morgan, Curtis yielded to economic necessity and at least bent the truth. He often stressed the importance of popular appeal in his imagery, yet the format he chose for *The North American Indian* dictated a price which betrayed that ideal. But in his visual imagery, Curtis went to great lengths to insure that it reflected his artistic sentiments truthfully, even when those sentiments reflected attitudes which we may now find repugnant.

Photographers often use their images to lie, but they are not the only ones whose use of photography can be deceitful. If one knowingly captions a photograph with a description which is untrue, the net effect of image and caption fulfills the intent to lie. A similar net effect may result from the juxtaposition of photographs, and in neither case need it be a photographer who creates the combination which lies. In presentations of photographs, again, it is the *intent* to deceive that defines lying.

Fiction, both verbal and visual, is different from lying in that it announces itself as a conscious creation of illusion. In an untitled image made in 1971, photographer Jerry Uelsmann depicts a giant hamburger, floating in a dramatically cloudy sky above deck chairs arranged on a beach. We are fooled by the absurd scale of this image just long enough to make us laugh when we recognize that it is the result of extreme but skillful manipulation of the photographic process. Uelsmann is no liar, but he has made a career out of the intentional creation of photographic fictions.

Intent, however, is often difficult to identify. Between hypothetical absolutes of fiction and of lying there is a continuous spectrum of variations in consciousness of intent. Attempts at communication inevitably—and often ambiguously—fall somewhere within this continuous spectrum. Curtis's photographs of Indians are among those which are ambiguous.

There is no doubt that Curtis intended his manipulation of subjects, and he was certainly aware of Adulf Muhr's retouching of his images. At the same time, however, he appears to have believed quite honestly that these manipulations were necessary to the truthful presentation of real "Indianness." On those occasions when he announced his imagery as reenactment—*In the Land of the Headhunters* being perhaps the best example—his work tended toward historical fiction. On other occasions, Curtis trumpeted the need to catch real "Indianness" quickly before it "vanished." But he *knew* that much of what he thought of as "Indianness" did not exist, and in that knowledge, his work tended toward deception.

Both in his photographs and in the text which accompanies them, Curtis frequently confused his biases with objective facts. That those biases—the obsession with "objective facts" primary among them—were often shared by his culture made such confusion all but invisible in Curtis's own time.

The existence of objective reality is an *a priori* concept. Being beyond proof, it can only be accepted or rejected on the basis of faith. As a product of our individual minds, the concept of objective reality is, however ironically, a subjective entity. While philosophers have accepted this paradox since before Socrates, its meaning is still debated and probably always will be. But I would assert that shared subjective perceptions are what have historically passed for objectivity. When one culture which shares a largely common subjectivity encounters another such culture, it has often led to the conflict of more than ideas. When one culture sees its difference from others in terms of hierarchical superiority, the failure to share their shared subjectivities has tended to lead to bloodshed. Thousands of Indians, who died at the hands of Whites justifying themselves under the delusion of Manifest Destiny, attested to this tendency with their deaths.

By the time Curtis began his work on *The North American Indian,* this obsession with racial bigotry was *beginning* to give way. Whites controlled the continent, and even in their continuing belief in the legitimacy of what we call racism, the weight of guilt was beginning to be felt. It was largely this guilt for what he described as "more than the crime of the century" that motivated Curtis's work.

In this age of modern communications, we are confronted with images of other cultures with increasing regularity. Photographs have been joined by television. Almost every time we watch the televised news, we are confronted by imagery of other cultures, often on the other side of the globe. When we confuse this imagery with reality, we run the risk of believing again that the values of our culture are "right" and that those of other cultures are "wrong." Our imagery through *whatever medium* shows us what we and our culture want to see.

Curtis's manipulations of his imagery, while they were essential to the power of his art, may make that imagery seem like a crude form of documentation when compared with the electronic immediacy of television. But even television, when a depiction of "Indiannesss" has been sought, has used Curtis's photographs for the purpose.

Only when we look at imagery of other cultures critically— whether it is Curtis's photographs of Indians, or television's video of people on the other side of the globe—can we hope to avoid lapsing again into stereotype. In the complexities of the modern world, we can no longer afford to allow our interactions with other cultures to be twisted by guilt. The tangle which results serves too often to perpetuate racism. Our criticism should be, in the words of Edward Curtis, "not in a spirit of faultfinding, but because the situation demands it."

Our criticism of imagery, furthermore, should not be limited to individual images, but should extend to sequences of images and the words which often accompany them. By doing so, we may hope to find that "one path towards error is closed and the road to truth is often at the same time opened."

1. Edward S. Curtis, *The North American Indian,* 20 vols. and port. (Privately printed, 1907-30), 5:xi.
2. Ann Horton, public address, Washington, D.C., March 28, 1981.
3. Dee Brown, *Bury My Heart at Wounded Knee: An Indian History of the American West,* 5th ed. (New York: Bantam Books, 1972), pp. 157-65.
4. Ibid., p. 417.
5. *Oxford English Dictionary,* s.v. "racism."
6. Charles Darwin, *The Descent of Man,* in *Darwin,* by Philip Appleman (New York: W. W. Norton & Co., 1979), p. 196.
7. Beaumont Newhall, *The History of Photography,* 4th ed. (New York: Museum of Modern Art, 1964), pp. 67-68.
8. Roy Meredith, *Mathew B. Brady: Mr. Lincoln's Camera Man,* 2d rev. ed. (New York: Dover Publications, 1974), pp. 83-93.
9. Oliver Wendell Holmes quoted in Robert Taft, *Photography and the American Scene* (1938; reprint ed., New York: Dover Publications, 1964), pp. 235-36.
10. Margaret Blackman, "Posing the American Indian," *Natural History* 89, no. 10 (October 1980):70.
11. Don D. Fowler and John F. Matley, *Material Culture of the Numa: The John Wesley Powell Collection, 1867-1880,* Smithsonian Contributions to Anthropology, no. 26 (Washington, D.C., 1979), p. 3.
12. Timo T. Pajunen, "Eadweard Muybridge," *Camera* 1 (1973):33.
13. Peter Palmquist, "Imagemakers of the Modoc War: Louis Heller and Eadweard Muybridge," *Journal of California Anthropology,* Winter 1977, pp. 211-37.
14. Taft, *Photography and the American Scene,* pp. 277-78.
15. Fredrick W. Hodge to Corrine Gilb, "Fredrick Webb Hodge, Ethnologist: A Tape Recorded Interview," 1954-56, photo copy of transcript in National Anthropological Archives, Smithsonian Institution, Washington, D.C., p. 72.
16. William Henry Fox Talbot, "The Process of Calotype Photogenic Drawing," 1841, in *Photography: Essays and Images,* Beaumont Newhall, ed. (New York: Museum of Modern Art, 1980), p. 33.
17. Taft, *Photography and the American Scene,* pp. 378-83.
18. Alexander Black, "The Amateur Photographer," 1887, in *Photography: Essays and Images,* Beaumont Newhall, ed. (New York: Museum of Modern Art, 1980), p. 150.
19. Brian Coe and Paul Gates, *The Snapshot Photograph: The Rise of Popular Photography* (London: Ash & Grant, 1977), p. 17.
20. Peter Henry Emerson, "Photography, A Pictorial Art," 1886, in *Photography: Essays and Images,* Beaumont Newhall, ed. (New York: Museum of Modern Art, 1980), p. 162.
21. Peter Galassi, *Before Photography: Painting and the Invention of Photography* (New York: Museum of Modern Art, 1981).
22. Lady Elizabeth Eastlake, "Photography," 1857, in *Photography: Essays and Images,* Beaumont Newhall, ed. (New York: Museum of Modern Art, 1980), p. 93.
23. William Innes Homer, *Alfred Stieglitz and the American Avant-Garde* (Boston: Little, Brown & Co., New York Graphic Society, 1979), pp. 11-12.
24. Alfred Stieglitz, "Pictorial Photography," 1899, in *Photography: Essays and Images,* Beaumont Newhall, ed. (New York: Museum of Modern Art, 1980), p. 163.
25. Ibid., p. 164.
26. Homer, *Stieglitz,* pp. 25-27.
27. Stieglitz, "Pictorial Photography," p. 167.
28. Bill Holm and George Irving Quimby, *Edward S. Curtis in the Land of the War Canoes: A Pioneer Cinematographer in the Pacific Northwest* (Seattle: University of Washington Press, 1980), p. 20.
29. Brown, *Wounded Knee,* pp. 38-65.
30. Holm and Quimby, *Land of the War Canoes,* p. 20.
31. *Argus,* December 19, 1896, p. 8. Clipping, Pacific Northwest Collection, University of Washington Libraries, Seattle.
32. Edward S. Curtis with Edward Marshall, "The Vanishing Red Man," *Hampton Magazine* 28, no. 4 (May 1912), p. 245.
33. Victor Boesen and Florence Curtis Graybill, *Edward Sheriff Curtis: Visions of a Vanishing Race* (New York: Thomas Y. Crowell Co., 1976), p. 9.
34. Alton A. Lindsey, "The Harriman Expedition to Alaska," *BioScience,* June 1978, p. 383.
35. Holm and Quimby, *Land of the War Canoes,* p. 20.
36. Edward S. Curtis, "The Amateur Photographer," *Western Trail* 1, no. 4 (February 1900):272, Pacific Northwest Collection.
37. Edward S. Curtis, "Photography," *Western Trail* 1, no. 3 (January 1900):187, Pacific Northwest Collection.
38. Curtis, "Amateur Photographer," p. 273, Pacific Northwest Collection.
39. Curtis, "Photography," p. 187, Pacific Northwest Collection.

40. "Convention Aftermath," *Camera Craft* 1, no. 5 (September 1900):268-69.

41. Curtis, "Amateur Photographer," p. 272, Pacific Northwest Collection.

42. Robert F. Berkhofer, *The White Man's Indian* (New York: Random House, Vintage Books, 1979), p. 94.

43. Darwin, *Descent of Man*, p. 198.

44. Ibid., p. 208.

45. Thomas F. Gossett, *Race: The History of an Idea in America* (New York: Schocken Books, 1965), p. 244.

46. Regna Diebold Darnell, "The Development of American Anthropology 1879-1920: From the Bureau of American Ethnology to Franz Boas" (Ph.D. diss., University of Pennsylvania, 1969), p. 24.

47. C. C. Royce, "Investigations Relating to the Cessions of Lands by Indian Tribes to the United States," *The First Annual Report of the Bureau of American Ethnology . . . Government Printing Office* (Washington, D.C.: Smithsonian Institution, 1881), p. 28.

48. Lewis Meriam, survey dir., *The Problem of Indian Administration* (Baltimore: Johns Hopkins Press, 1928).

49. Weston J. Naef, *The Collection of Alfred Stieglitz: Fifty Pioneers of Modern Photography* (New York: Viking Press, Metropolitan Museum of Art, 1978), p. 365.

50. Personal communication between Toby Quitslund and the author, June 25, 1981.

51. Arnold Genthe, "A Critical Review of the Salon Pictures with a Few Words upon the Tendency of the Photographers," *Camera Craft* 2, no. 4 (February 1901), p. 310.

52. "Edward S. Curtis: Photohistorian of the North American Indian," *Seattle Times*, November 15, 1903, magazine section. Clipping, Pacific Northwest Collection.

53. Robert Bigart and Clarence Woodcock, "The Rinehart Photographs: A Portfolio," *Montana the Magazine of Western History* 39, no. 4 (October 1979):24.

54. *Camera Craft* 13, no. 2 (1906), p. 308.

55. "Curtis' Indians," undated advertising pamphlet, Historical Photography Collection, University of Washington Libraries, Seattle.

56. Curtis to Hodge, October 28, 1904, Fredrick Webb Hodge Papers, Southwest Museum, Los Angeles, Calif.

57. Holm and Quimby, *Land of the War Canoes*, p. 25.

58. Gossett, *Race*, p. 238.

59. Ibid., p. 114.

60. "Will Sell Curtis Pictures: John C. Slater Leaves Seattle Tonight," *Seattle Times*, June 11, 1905. Clipping, Pacific Northwest Collection.

61. Walcott to Dinwiddie, April 16, 1907, Smithsonian Institution Archives, Washington, D.C.

62. Roosevelt to Curtis, December 16, 1905, Edward S. Curtis Materials, The Pierpont Morgan Library, New York, N.Y.

63. Boesen and Graybill, *Curtis*, p. 20.

64. Curtis to Morgan, January 23, 1906, Curtis Materials.

65. Curtis to Bella de Costa Greene, April 6, 1914, Curtis Materials.

66. Curtis to Hodge, April 25, 1906, Hodge Papers.

67. Curtis, *North American Indian*, 1:Introduction.

68. Theodore Roosevelt, Foreword to *North American Indian*.

69. "Will Show Them This Week: Exhibit of the New Curtis Indian Prints," *Seattle Times*, July 12, 1903. Clipping, Pacific Northwest Collection.

70. George Wharton James, "The Study of Indian Faces," *Camera Craft* 8, no. 1 (December 1903), p. 13.

71. "A Seattle Man's Triumph," *Seattle Times*, May 22, 1904. Clipping, Pacific Northwest Collection.

72. Personal communication between Lee and the author, August 11, 1980.

73. Taft, *Photography and the American Scene*, p. 323.

74. A. F. Muhr, "A Gum Bichromate Process for Obtaining Colored Prints from a Single Negative," *Camera Craft* 8, no. 2 (August 1906), p. 280.

75. Curtis to Hodge, August 25, 1907, Hodge Papers.

76. Hodge to Gilb, p. 104.

77. Curtis to Hodge, December 17, 1907, Hodge Papers.

78. Curtis to Edmund S. Meany, November 11, 1907, Edmund S. Meany Papers, Archives and Records Center, University of Washington, Seattle.

79. Curtis to Hodge, December 26, 1907, Hodge Papers.

80. Ibid., December 27, 1907.

81. Curtis, *North American Indian*, 1:16.

82. Ibid., p. 38.

83. Ibid., p. 75.

84. Ibid., pp. 21-22.

85. Edward S. Curtis, "Vanishing Indian Types: The Tribes of the Northwest Plains," *Scribner's Magazine* 39, no. 6 (June 1906), p. 660.

86. Gossett, *Race*, pp. 71-83.

87. Curtis, *North American Indian*, 2:xii.

88. Ibid., p. 48.

89. Ibid., p. 50.

90. Ibid., p. 48.

91. Ibid., p. 65.

92. Curtis, "Vanishing Indian Types," p. 657.

93. Curtis, *North American Indian*, 3:xiii.

94. Ibid., p. xi.

95. Ibid., p. xi-xii.

96. Ibid., p. 5.

97. Curtis to Hodge, January 14, 1908, Hodge Papers.

98. Curtis, *North American Indian,* 4:xi.

99. Robert H. Lowie, *The Crow Indians* (New York: Rinehart & Co., 1935), p. 355.

100. Boesen and Graybill, *Curtis,* pp. 27-40.

101. Curtis to Meany, July 31, 1908, Meany Papers.

102. Curtis, *North American Indian,* 5:xii.

103. Ibid., 6:xi.

104. Ibid., p. 8.

105. Ibid., 3:6.

106. Curtis to Greene, March 21, 1913, Curtis Materials.

107. Curtis to Hodge, July 21, 1910, Hodge Papers.

108. Curtis to Meany, November 19, 1911, Meany Papers.

109. Ibid.

110. Curtis to Hodge, January 14, 1912, Hodge Papers.

111. Theater bill, Historical Photography Collection.

112. Curtis, *North American Indian,* 9:Preface.

113. Holm and Quimby, *Land of the War Canoes,* pp. 29-30.

114. Curtis, *North American Indian,* 9:xi-xii.

115. Boesen and Graybill, *Curtis,* p. 28.

116. Curtis to Hodge, December 27, 1909, Hodge Papers.

117. Blackman, "Posing the American Indian," p. 71.

118. Sheets to Morgan, August 2, 1915; and draft letter, Morgan to Sheets, August 16, 1915, Curtis Materials.

119. Curtis to Hodge, February 19, 1913; February 24, 1913; April 1, 1914, Hodge Papers.

120. Curtis to Meany, April 20, 1914, Meany Papers.

121. "Edward S. Curtis Cited for Contempt," *Seattle Times,* June 19, 1918. Clipping, Pacific Northwest Collection.

122. Boesen and Graybill, *Curtis,* p. 88.

123. Curtis, *North American Indian,* 12:xi.

124. George Wharton James, "The Snake Dance of the Hopis," *Camera Craft* 6, no. 1 (November 1902):7-8.

125. Curtis to Hodge, November 28, 1924, Hodge Papers.

126. Curtis to Meany, October 8, 1922, Meany Papers.

127. Curtis, *North American Indian,* 13:xi-xii.

128. Ibid., 15:xi.

129. Ibid., 16:xi.

130. Ibid., p. 12.

131. Ibid., 17:xi.

132. Ibid., 18:xi.

133. Ibid., xii.

134. Hodge to Curtis, May 19, 1927, Hodge Papers.

135. Curtis to Hodge, December 7, 1927, Hodge Papers.

136. Ibid.

137. *Seattle Post Intelligencer,* October 12, 1927. Pacific Northwest Collection.

138. Curtis to Greene, April 20, 1932, Curtis Materials.

139. J. C. Warburg, "Photography and Natural Selection," *Camera Work* 6 (April 1904):23.

140. Roy Emerson Stryker and Nancy Wood, *In This Proud Land: America 1935-1943 As Seen in the FSA Photographs* (Boston: New York Graphic Society, 1975, c. 1973).

141. Susan Sontag, *On Photography* (New York: Farrar, Straus & Giroux, Delta, 1977), p. 62.

CHRONOLOGY

1868	Born in rural Wisconsin.
1887	Moved to Seattle with his family.
1891	Went into business with a partner as "photographers and photo-engravers."
1896	Won bronze medal from the Photographers' Association of America for "excellency in posing, lighting and tone."
1897	Went into business on his own; his reputation as a commercial photographer of romantic portraits and landscapes grew.
1898	Took first photographs of Indians as part of the local scenery.
1899	Accompanied E. H. Harriman Expedition to Alaska as official photographer; met important natural scientists; began relationship with the Harrimans which led to contact with major political and business figures in the Northeast.
1900	Stayed with George Bird Grinnell as a guest on the Crow Indian Reservation in Montana; decided to devote himself full time to photographing Indians. Made first trip to the Southwest later in the year.
1900-1906	Worked as businessman and full-time photographer of Indians (before publication of *The North American Indian*). Photographed extensively among the tribes of the Southwest, Great Plains, and Pacific Northwest. Established basic elements of style and approach to photographing Indians. Hired large staff to assist in darkroom work, field work, and publicity. Supported himself through private altruism and "business energy." Made many and probably most of the photographs eventually used in *The North American Indian*.
1905	Met President Theodore Roosevelt, who became ardent fan and helped with public relations and fundraising.
1906	Convinced J. Pierpont Morgan to provide capital loan to begin publication of *The North American Indian*.
1907	Published volume one of *The North American Indian*.
1910-1912	Devoted winters full time to fundraising because of financial problems. Created multimedia extravaganza *Curtis Indian Picture Opera*.
1913	Published in volume nine a tribute to J. P. Morgan upon his death. Secured further support from Morgan's son for *The North American Indian*.
1916-1922	Stalled publication of *The North American Indian*.
1922-1926	Made some of his most artistic photographs in California; finished volumes on the Southwest and northern Midwest, often using photographs made earlier.
1927	Made photographs in Oklahoma and Alaska, some of which are relatively unmanipulative of his subjects or the photographic process.
1930	Published volume twenty of *The North American Indian*. Suffered from depression and his work lapsed into obscurity.
1952	Died at his daughter's home in Los Angeles.
late 1960-early 1970s	His photographs reemerge on a wave of popularity of modern "noble-savagism" and become the most famous historical photographs of Indian subjects.

BIBLIOGRAPHY

Books

Appleman, Philip. *Darwin*. 2d ed. New York: W. W. Norton & Co., 1979.

Berkhofer, Robert F. *The White Man's Indian*. New York: Random House, Vintage Books, 1979.

Boesen, Victor, and Graybill, Florence Curtis. *Edward Sheriff Curtis: Visions of a Vanishing Race*. New York: Thomas Y. Crowell Co., 1976.

Brown, Dee. *Bury My Heart at Wounded Knee: An Indian History of the American West*. 5th ed. New York: Bantam Books, 1972.

Coe, Brian, and Gates, Paul. *The Snapshot Photograph: The Rise of Popular Photography 1888-1939*. London: Ash & Grant, 1977.

Curtis, Edward S. *The North American Indian*. 20 vols. and port. Privately printed, 1907-30.

Darnell, Regna Diebold. "The Development of American Anthropology 1879-1920: From the Bureau of American Ethnology to Franz Boas." Ph.D. dissertation, University of Pennsylvania, 1969.

Dorsey, George A. *Indians of the Southwest*. Passenger Department, Atchinson, Topeka & Santa Fe Railway System, 1903.

Fowler, Don D., and Matley, John F. *Material Culture of the Numa: The John Wesley Powell Collection, 1867-1880*. Smithsonian Contributions to Anthropology, no. 26. Washington, D.C., 1979.

"Fredrick Webb Hodge, Ethnologist: A Tape Recorded Interview." Photo copy of a transcript in National Anthropological Archives, Smithsonian Institution, Washington, D.C.

Galassi, Peter. *Before Photography: Painting and the Invention of Photography*. New York: Museum of Modern Art, 1981.

Gossett, Thomas F. *Race: The History of an Idea in America*. New York: Schocken Books, 1965.

Holm, Bill, and Quimby, George Irving. *Edward S. Curtis in the Land of the War Canoes: A Pioneer Cinematographer in the Pacific Northwest*. Seattle: University of Washington Press, 1980.

Homer, William Innes. *Alfred Stieglitz and the American Avant-Garde*. Boston: Little, Brown & Co., New York Graphic Society, 1979.

Lowie, Robert H. *The Crow Indians*. New York: Rinehart & Co., 1935.

Meredith, Roy. *Mathew B. Brady: Mr. Lincoln's Camera Man*. 2d rev. ed. New York: Dover Publications, 1974.

Meriam, Lewis, survey dir. *The Problem of Indian Administration*. Baltimore: Johns Hopkins Press, 1928.

Naef, Weston J. *The Collection of Alfred Stieglitz: Fifty Pioneers of Modern Photography*. New York: Viking Press, Metropolitan Museum of Art, 1978.

Newhall, Beaumont. *The History of Photography*. 4th ed. New York: Museum of Modern Art, 1964.

————, ed. *Photography: Essays & Images*. New York: Museum of Modern Art, 1980.

Royce, C. C. "Investigations Relating to the Cessions of Lands by Indian Tribes to the United States." *The First Annual Report of the Bureau of American Ethnology . . . Government Printing Office*. Washington, D.C.: Smithsonian Institution, 1881.

Sontag, Susan. *On Photography*. New York: Farrar, Straus & Giroux, Delta, 1977.

Stryker, Roy Emerson, and Wood, Nancy. *In This Proud Land: America 1935-1943 As Seen in the FSA Photographs*. Boston: New York Graphic Society, 1975, c. 1973.

Taft, Robert. *Photography and the American Scene*. 1938. Reprint. New York: Dover Publications, 1964.

Periodicals

Argus, December 19, 1896. Pacific Northwest Collection, University of Washington Libraries, Seattle.

Curtis, Edward S. "Photography." *Western Trail* 1, no. 3 (January 1900):186-88. Pacific Northwest Collection, University of Washington Libraries, Seattle.

————. "The Amateur Photographer." *Western Trail* 1, no. 4 (February 1900):272-74. Pacific Northwest Collection, University of Washington Libraries, Seattle.

156

"Convention Aftermath." *Camera Craft* 1, no. 5 (September 1900):269.

Genthe, Arnold. "A Critical Review of the Salon Pictures with a Few Words upon the Tendency of the Photographers." *Camera Craft* 2, no. 4 (February 1901):310.

James, George Wharton. "The Snake Dance of the Hopis." *Camera Craft* 6, no. 1 (November 1902):3-10.

Curtis, Edward S., with Marshall, Edward. "The Vanishing Red Man." *Hampton Magazine* 28, no. 4 (December 1903):245.

Warburg, J. C. "Photography and Natural Selection." *Camera Work* 6 (April 1904):23.

James, George Wharton. "The Study of Indian Faces." *Camera Craft* 8, no. 1 (1906).

Curtis, Edward S. "Vanishing Indian Types: The Tribes of the Northwest Plains." *Scribner's Magazine* 39, no. 6 (June 1906):657-71.

Muhr, A. F. "A Gum Bichromate Process for Obtaining Colored Prints from a Single Negative." *Camera Craft* 8, no 2 (August 1906):278-81.

Pajunen, Timo T. "Eadweard Muybridge." *Camera* 1 (1973):33.

Palmquist, Peter. "Imagemakers of the Modoc War: Louis Heller and Eadweard Muybridge." *Journal of California Anthropology,* Winter 1977.

Lindsey, Alton A. "The Harriman Expedition to Alaska." *BioScience,* June 1978, pp. 384-86.

Bigart, Robert, and Woodcock, Clarence. "The Rinehart Photographs: A Portfolio." *Montana the Magazine of Western History* 39, no. 4 (October 1979):24.

Blackman, Margaret. "Posing the American Indian." *Natural History* 89, no. 10 (October 1980):68-74.

Newspapers

"Will Show Them This Week: Exhibit of the New Curtis Indian Prints." *Seattle Times,* July 12, 1903. Pacific Northwest Collection, University of Washington Libraries, Seattle.

"Edward S. Curtis: Photohistorian of the North American Indian." *Seattle Times,* November 15, 1903, magazine section. Pacific Northwest Collection, University of Washington Libraries, Seattle.

"A Seattle Man's Triumph." *Seattle Times,* May 22, 1904. Pacific Northwest Collection, University of Washington Libraries, Seattle.

"Will Sell Curtis Pictures: John C. Slater Leaves Seattle Tonight." *Seattle Times,* June 11, 1905. Pacific Northwest Collection, University of Washington Libraries, Seattle.

"Edward S. Curtis Cited for Contempt." *Seattle Times,* June 19, 1918. Pacific Northwest Collection, University of Washington Libraries, Seattle.

Unpublished Sources

Los Angeles, California
Southwest Museum. Fredrick Webb Hodge Papers.

New York, New York
The Pierpont Morgan Library. Edward Curtis Materials.

Seattle, Washington
University of Washington Libraries: Historical Photography Collection, Pacific Northwest Collection.
University Archives and Records Center. Edmund S. Meany Papers.

Washington, D.C.
Smithsonian Institution Archives.

INDEX OF IMAGES

Numbers refer to illustration number.

158